Twayne's English Authors Series

Sylvia E. Bowman, *Editor*

INDIANA UNIVERSITY

Robert Browning

 168

Robert Browning

Robert Browning

By ROBERT BRAINARD PEARSALL

College of Notre Dame

TWAYNE PUBLISHERS
A DIVISION OF G. K. HALL & CO., BOSTON

Library of Congress Cataloging in Publication Data

Pearsall, Robert Brainard, 1920–
  Robert Browning.

  (Twayne's English authors series, TEAS 168)
  Bibliography: p. 183.
  1. Browning, Robert, 1812–1889—Criticism and
interpretation.
PR4238.P37   821'.8   73-20388
ISBN 0-8057-1065-5

Lovingly
Dedicated to

MADELEINE PEARSALL

Contents

Preface

In 1880, a full decade before the death of the poet, Browning Clubs and Browning Societies began to spring up in the major cities of Britain and America. In the years between 1890 and 1914 there were thousands of such organizations, and it was possible to speak of a Browning Movement just as one might speak of a Socialist Movement or Christian Science Movement. To some extent the work of these groups was proselytory and pious: Browning had had a good deal to say about the most troublesome religious and philosophic problems of his day, and could be presented as a teacher, a seer, a prophet. Writing in the *Century Magazine* in 1883, an American critic noted that Browning spoke "with authority, and not as the Scribes and Pharisees." People trusted, said the reviewer, "the comprehensive views he takes on a subject," the "reserve power that seems to exist behind all his works," and the ability to teach by suggestion, so that "the best in him is something that hardly comes to the consciousness of the reader, though it influences him profoundly."

But to the needs of discipleship implicit in this view, there were added needs of explanation and interpretation; for Browning, like many another seer and oracle, had a habit of not making himself clear. "He has veiled himself in a language often obscure, often rough and discursive to the verge of unintelligibility, sometimes odd to the perilous point of mannerism," said the same critic in the *Century Magazine*. Browning was great; he was rewarding; more than any other poet, ever, he stirred the minds of great masses of contemporary readers. But he was "obscure," and needed not only to be read but to be studied. It was the study of Browning and not the proselytizing of him that became the main work of the Browning groups all over the world.

Although I personally believe that Browning was one of the most satisfactory public voices of recent centuries, I have not made any such claim in this book. The purpose of the book is simply to explain. I have tried to provide a straightforward account of Browning's poetic career as a whole, to give special attention to works and issues of special interest, and to gloss with cogent events in the life of the poet. Despite awareness of the dangers, I have hoped to say something useful or interesting about every book and every poem that Browning published. And at the very least, I do place every book and poem at its appropriate position in the poet's life and work, and suggest why it is to be found just there. In a book of this scope it is often impossible to give a full justification of qualitative evaluations, or even of explicative ones, but I have done what I could to explain my judgments under both heads. Chapter divisions in the book key to the sequence in which Browning wrote and published his thirty volumes of poetry; but sometimes, especially in the later chapters, I have been able to group works by genre without significant sacrifice of continuity.

My quotations are from texts edited by F. G. Kenyon in *The Works of Robert Browning*, first published in 1912 by Smith, Elder, and Co., London, and published since 1966 by Barnes and Noble, New York. I have checked for significant variant readings in early volumes of *The Complete Works of Robert Browning*, a variorum edition now being published (in thirteen volumes) under the general editorship of Roma A. King, Jr. by the Ohio University Press. For assistance in matters great and small I gladly offer thanks to staffs and governing boards of the Bodley Library, Oxford; the British Museum Library; the New York Public Library; the libraries of the University of Texas, University of Michigan, and University of California at Berkeley and at Los Angeles; and the Henry E. Huntington Museum and Library. Kind thanks to Mary Elizabeth Fry, June Moll, Warren Roberts, and Harold Ericson, and to the whole race of librarians which they represent. Kind thanks to Sylvia Bowman, Mary Ellen Boyling, Marilyn Meyer Pearsall, Barbara Klinefelter, Gae Holladay, and Arlene Epp, for miscellaneous but most needed help.

ROBERT BRAINARD PEARSALL

College of Notre Dame
Belmont, California

Chronology

1849	His son, Robert Weideman Barrett Browning, born in Florence.
1850	April 1, publishes *Christmas Eve and Easter Day*.
1855	November 17, publishes *Men and Women* in two volumes.
1861	June 29, Elizabeth Barrett Browning dies in Florence. Begins his twenty-six-year residence in Warwick Crescent, London.
1864	Publishes *Dramatis Personae*. Advances in London society.
1871	Publishes *Balaustion's Adventure*. Publishes *Prince Hohenstiel-Schwangau*.
1872	Publishes *Fifine at the Fair*. Continental traveling.
1873	Publishes *Red-Cotton Nightcap Country*. Moves to international society.
1875	Publishes *Aristophanes' Apology*. Publishes *The Inn Album* in the *New York Times*, then in book form.
1876	Publishes *Pacchiarotto and How He Worked in Distemper*.
1877	Publishes The *Agamemnon of Aeschylus*.
1878	In one volume, publishes *La Saisiaz* and *The Two Poets of Croisic*.
1879	Publishes *Dramatic Idyls*.
1880	Publishes *Dramatic Idyls, Second Series*. Establishment of the Browning Society in London, and of worldwide Browning "movement."
1883	Publishes *Jocoseria*. Son advances as a painter.
1884	Publishes *Ferishtah's Fancies*.
1887	Publishes *Parleyings with Certain People*. Commences edition of his complete works. Son marries an American heiress.
1889	Completes edition. Publishes *Asolando: Fancies and Facts*. On December 12, dies in his son's palazzo in Venice. December 31, buried in Westminster Abbey.

CHAPTER 1

Young Browning

I The World in 1812

ROBERT Browning was born in Camberwell, a prosperous and comparatively rural suburb of London, on May 7, 1812. The place and year have their significance. Until 1812 the question of European supremacy, which implied world supremacy, had not been settled; nor, within Britain itself, had the question of political and economic leadership been settled. But by 1812 the saga of Napoleon and the thrust for world leadership were over for the French. Other nations of Europe, exhausted and bled white, in various stages of national disgrace, floundered through wars, revolutions, and redrawings of borders—Spain and Poland were all but extinguished; Germany and Italy had not been created; Russia was not interested in matters beyond her own vast territories. Africa, Asia, and the Americas, which had not developed at an equal pace with Europe, had lost their ancient significance without taking on their modern one. Their interim role was to provide theaters for British leadership and markets for British commerce and industry. In technology, management, and finance, the Britons were the most successful of human beings, and the most admired.

At their commercial center, and therefore at the center of the world, sprawled the city of London. London, which already covered hundreds of square miles, was exploding outward through scores of new suburbs every year. At the center of London, in an ancient street picturesquely called Threadneedle, sprawled the Bank of England. A strange entity, half-private and half-national, cumbrous, complicated, and inert-seeming, the Bank deployed so much power as to influence

events in every part of the globe. For more than eighty years,
neither nation nor city nor bank was to have any serious rival.
Browning, who was to live nearly eighty years, who often
made fun of all three, and who claimed, sometimes, a spiritual
citizenship in Italy or "the world," was nevertheless intimately
related to England, I ondon, and the Bank of England.

II *Menage in Camberwell*

The poet's grandfather, the first Robert Browning to reside
in London, had risen from nothing to a lucrative head clerkship
in the Bank of England, and thereby founded the solid respectability of the family. An aggressive, no-nonsense man, he also
advanced himself by marriage to a Creole lady, Margaret
Tittle, heiress to plantation properties on the island of St. Kitts.
To them were born two children, one of whom, Robert II,
was to become the father of the poet. The character of Robert
II was softer than that of his father. He was tender, bookish,
imaginative, often outlandish in his behavior, a seeker of the
odd and grotesque, lovable enough, but a strange character.
After two youthful bad experiences, one as clerk in the brutal
environment of a slave-worked plantation on St. Kitts, the other
in a passionate attempt to become a painter, he sorrowfully
followed his tougher father into the great bank.

Considerable pathos exists in the various other attempts of
the soft son to repeat the deeds of the hard father. Robert
I had moved from the city to the suburb of Peckham; Robert
II moved as soon as possible to the neighboring suburb, Camberwell. Robert I had married an exotic from the Caribbean;
the wife of Robert II was Scottish, and doubly foreign since
her father was a German. Robert I found a second wife soon
after the death of his first, and so did Robert II. But Robert
II did not rise in the bank as his father had done; and his
outland wife was not even stylish, let alone an heiress. His
attempt at a second marriage was not masterful and fruitful,
as his father's had been; it was a ludicrous fiasco which left
him bankrupt and exiled. His fine skills in languages and history wasted themselves in the pursuit of historical titbits and
curiosa; he devoted his excellent draftsmanship to chilling
little profiles and naughty cartoons; in him those dreams of
power which all men have, and which his father had built
up as an actual power, crumbled to the study of necromancy

and torture systems, and to the surgical autopsies he continually performed on small animals.

Both the purposeful grandfather and the ineffectual father
were available for the contemplation of Robert III, the child
born in 1812; but Sarah Anna Weidermann Browning, the
poet's mother, was more important than either of the men.
Except for its library, the home at Camberwell was her castle
rather than her husband's. Rather than moving into the native
Church of England, her husband's church, she remained a
Scottish Congregationalist; and she led her family to chapel
on all possible occasions. She was devoted to gardening and
the piano, and undoubtedly laid the groundwork for her son's
excellent knowledge of flowers and musical techniques. In
other ways, she may not have been wholly satisfactory. Alexandra Orr, Browning's most knowledgeable early biographer,
says tartly that, "in all her goodness and sweetness she seems
to have been somewhat matter-of-fact."[1] She had no imaginative scope, and little sympathy for views not held by herself.

There seems scarcely any doubt that her son put Sarah Anna
in the paternal rather than in the maternal position, that he
feared as well as loved her, and that many of the less satisfactory
aspects of his work arose from a subconscious or semiconscious
desire to say what he wished to say without offending an
authority-figure who would not have wished him to say it.
Betty Miller, in her interesting biography of the poet, goes
much farther, arguing that the whole range of Browning's
human relationships was skewed off center by the vesting
of authority in this rather tight and narrow woman.[2] That she
temporarily controlled both Robert II and Robert III is very
certain. Her daughter, Sarianna, naturally grew up in conscious
imitation. Their cousin Cyrus Mason maliciously noted
Sarianna's habit of strutting ostentatiously to Chapel, while
a cowed housemaid, two paces behind her, carried her prayer-
book.

These four, Robert II, Robert III, Sarah Anna, and Sarianna,
made up an oddly assorted but generally winsome little household. Onlookers who were not friends sometimes found them
egotistical and opinionated; and even Thomas Carlyle, who
loved and admired the young Browning, found him full of
"cockney self-regard" which he blamed on the family. As he
matured, Browning became scrupulous in the stance and lan-

guage of the leisured classes. In middle life he sometimes
had a dubiously concocted coat-of-arms printed on his note
paper, and his son Robert IV, called "Pen," always did. But
the Brownings in the eighty years of British supremacy were
exactly of the respectable middle classes which had become
supreme in Britain. No family could have been more of its
place and time than that of Robert Browning.

III   *Seedtime in the Suburbs*

Browning's infancy and childhood were generally pleasant
when he was at home and unpleasant when he was in school.
Of course, his schools were not of the best. The old universities were barred to him because of his mother's Calvinist
strictness; and Robert Browning II, an Anglican born, neither
caused his wife to say the one word that was necessary, nor
said the one word himself. The father's timidity probably did
the son a disservice. The great teacher Benjamin Jowett, writing long afterward, explained to Lady Tennyson his own
estimate of Browning. Browning's literary faults, said Jowett,
"at first sprang from carelessness and an uncritical habit, and
are now born and bred within him. He has no form, or has
it only by accident when the subject is limited."[3] Carefulness
in details, critical awareness, and a taste for structure are
exactly the qualities a good school would have worked to produce. Above all such a school would have produced in Browning a regard for competition within set rules, and a more intelligent awareness of the needs of people around him.

The schools Browning did attend were pulpit-oriented
extempore affairs, lacking both past and future, but at that
time well-patronized and flourishing. Browning, who had
learned to read at home, had accumulated the store of discon-
nected knowledge which is the treasure of bookish children.
The school routines bored and disgusted him. By his own
account, his precocity caused trouble by humiliating other children; he unquestionably put on airs, and got himself disliked
by the other children.

He says [wrote his old friend Alfred Domett] they taught him nothing
there, and that he was bullied by the big boys. When first there,

at eight or nine years of age, he says he made a copy of verses . . .
intended to ingratiate himself with the master, a Mr. Ready. He quoted
the two concluding lines, which ran thus:—

> We boys are privates in our Regiment's ranks—
> 'Tis to our Captain that we owe all thanks.

—a compliment to the master, which got him favored in his school
exercises for some time, and enabled him to play with impunity little
impudent tricks, such as shutting the master's lexicon when his head
was turned away . . . to give him the trouble of hunting up a word
again.[4]

For the rest of his life Browning's feeling for the school was
summed up in the word "disgust."

At fourteen the boy had had enough, and dropped out in
favor of two more years of reading and private studies. Though
denying his son a chance at the great schools because of his
wife's scruples, Robert Browning II was unflaggingly generous
in providing a substitute education. Browning enjoyed the
help of a string of private tutors of the intelligent and agreeable
kind who flock to prosperous suburbs. From his tutors he
learned riding, boxing, dancing, fencing, and a great deal of
art and music, as well as French, Italian, and German. In 1828,
when he was sixteen, he entered the newly founded University
College, the nucleus of London University. Established as
a nonsectarian foundation, the University was trying to support
itself by a subscription system, each subscription set to cost
a hundred pounds (or four thousand dollars in modern cur-
rency), and to provide four years of prepaid tuition to a person
nominated by the subscriber. Browning II subscribed in favor
of Browning III, and established him in rooms in Bedford
Square near the university. But home still seemed best. Within
two weeks Browning had dropped out entirely and had returned to his own house and its succession of friendly tutors.

And, of course, he also returned to the library. In "Development," Browning pictures his father as a teacher so perfect as to organize instruction in "The Tale of Troy" all the
way from acting it out with chairs and tables to the real philolog-
ical study of Homer's Greek. Actually no developmental pat-
tern can be found in the known reading of Robert III. Certain
titles have quite fortuitously come to the front: Francis

Quarles's *Emblems*, Daniel Defoe's *Robinson Crusoe*, Alexander Pope's *Homer*, Christopher Smart's *Song of David*. The Bible, Shakespeare, and Milton were taken for granted. The boy read such things with extreme empathy, often identifying himself with tormented animals or with people in prison. He early developed an affection for a strange old folio volume called *Wanley's Wonders of the Little World* (1678), an enormous collection of instances of oddity, pain, violence, and humiliation—a perfect treasury of things one would hate to have happen to oneself. As any child might do, he gloated over the flesh-hooks in the palace basement, the king with the warped legs, the failed singer, and the lascivious bishop. He developed a good habit of cross-reading, often following items found in an independent volume through to the *Biographie Universelle*, an encyclopedia of fifty volumes, his favorite reference work. Connected history did not interest the young Browning. He liked to contemplate individual humans, and like most readers found special interest in individuals who were in trouble.

This kind of reading—wayward, unsystematic, personally involved, focused upon painful event and isolated personality—had an immeasurable effect on Browning's poetry. Less significant over the long run was his discovery of Shelley. Shelley, who had been safely dead for five years, was just then rising into apotheosis. The fourteen-year-old Browning, "thunderstruck" by Shelley, was by no means alone. From the brilliant Romantic poet, Browning learned a number of discrete ideas such as atheism, vegetarianism, social consciousness, and the self-immolating missions which may become the lot of master spirits. For some time the boy was a vegetarian, and, though he did not tell his mother, he was also an atheist. But the effects of exposure to Shelley soon sloughed off, leaving only *Pauline* and some complementary short poems to mark their passing.

IV   *Some Circles and the Set*

After the family and school have tried, a man is educated by his friends. Browning's middle-aged decades as "the greatest diner-out in London" were foreshadowed by his gregarious boyhood and youth. He was what Samuel Johnson called "a clubbable man"; he enjoyed friendships and friendly groups for their own sakes, and he liked to combine social with intellectual pleasures when possible.

The first of the informal circles in which he moved was led by Benjamin Flower and W. J. Fox as significant males and by Eliza and Sarah Flower as significant females. Flower was a liberal reformer whose brilliant editing of the *Cambridge Intelligencer* had ended in imprisonment for libel. The thrusting, self-made, ex-weaver Fox, who had become his disciple, was a prosperous Unitarian preacher, an aggressive journalist, and a rising politician who was destined to achieve a powerful voice in the House of Commons. To Eliza Flower, years earlier, Browning had first shown a stitched-together manuscript volume he called *Incondita*, and she had urged him to continue as a poet. He was fourteen then, and she twenty-three; but their connection was close, and she is the probable inspirer of *Pauline*. Sarah Flower, Eliza's sister, was also sympathetic to Browning. In one long conversation with her he brought the atheistical arguments of Shelley, or perhaps Voltaire, so powerfully into play as to shake her faith and leave her sleepless that night. A learned and productive musician, Sarah recovered to write the celebrated hymn "Nearer My God to Thee."

From this circle, Browning also had his first experience of what were then called "unconventional relationships." Eliza Flower, already the ward of Fox, had become his admirer and probable mistress. Mrs. Fox objected; and, after much agony on all sides, Eliza became Fox's housekeeper in a new home, farther out in the suburbs. Among Fox's friends were John Stuart Mill and Harriet Taylor, whose long liaison would also have been of great interest to Browning. Through his contact with the Flower-Fox circle, Browning came into successive contact with the political scientist Mill, the actor-manager Charles Macready, and the journalist James Forster, all of whom later affected his destiny. Through these acquaintances he met still more notable men—Carlyle, William Wordsworth, and Walter Savage Landor, whom he afterwards sheltered in Italy. At Macready's country house, too, he met Euphrasia Haworth, the literary lady, eleven years older than he, who replaced Miss Flower as his confidential female friend and who also wrote the earliest of the thousands of poems which have been written in praise of Browning. The first of her "Sonnets to the Author of *Paracelsus*," published in the

New Monthly Magazine for September, 1836, begins with lines
that have become well known:

> He has the quiet and calm look of one
> Who is assured of genius too intense
> To doubt of its own power.

Browning responded pleasantly by enshrining her as "My
English Eyebright" in a paragraph among the couplets of *Sordello*. Their affection continued until 1845, when she was replaced in her turn by Elizabeth Barrett.

Another group of friends, and in the long run the most satisfactory, was comprised of cheerful, lively, ambitious, but basically uncreative young men, merchants' sons now busily
advancing themselves as professional men. Unlike the looser
groups of artists and subintellectuals, they had a rather strict
identity and called themselves by the club-names "Set" and
"Colloquials." The Set yachted, danced, hiked, read, sketched,
and planned governments; and in its good-natured way represented an abyss of dilettantism. Only after the Set dispersed
did its members begin to accomplish things. Alfred Domett,
the member of the group to whom Browning was most warmly
attached, went to New Zealand, where he rose to a brief tenure
as Prime Minister. Joseph Arnould, who had won the New-
digate Prize at Oxford, pursued a double career as barrister
and journalist, wrote the authoritative legal volumes on Marine
Insurance, and became "Sir Joseph Arnould" as judge of the
High Court in Bombay. Lesser names of the group were William Young, Charles Dowson, and Browning's dear friend
Christopher Dowson. Young and the Dowsons were scions
of minor maritime capitalists living at the then pleasant little
river-port of Limehouse. One older man, a Captain Pritchard,
served as the elder statesman of the Set. A "brisk, dapper,
little, grey-haired sea-captain, with a squint and a delightful
fund of tales of adventure," he enjoyed helping out the young
people. It was he who arranged to have Browning attend sur-
gery classes at Guy's Hospital; and he left Sarianna Browning
the very large sum of a thousand pounds when he died.

These were sentimental as well as holiday attachments for
Browning. In their correspondence to and about each other
the young men liked to use fondling phrases like "Dear, dear

X," and *"Carissimi Amici."* They tended to regard friendship as a deliberate and permanent construct rather than a thing of accident and chance. They blocked off much of English life, since the lower and lower-middle classes were excluded from their interests and since they generally distrusted the upper classes. None was what might be called intellectual. But within these limitations they were a high-spirited and attractive group. Unlike the sets of literary people, they were secure in status and in well-being. Among the Set, Browning was easy and comfortable, and without exception the men in this group remained his friends for life.

V *Into Poetry*

Browning's failure to remain in the university or, afterwards, to suggest any useful alternative, somewhat distressed his father and mother. A generation earlier, when Robert II had expressed his desire to become an artist, the fierce Robert I had disowned him, and broken off relations until he was well into his career in the Bank of England. The gentler Robert II expressed some worry, but then settled back to wait for the decision to be made by Robert III. Sarah Anna expressed her unhappiness more vigorously. She had wanted her son to become a barrister like Alfred Domett, whom she admired, and failing that, she wanted him to have a business career, probably in the Bank. Her notion of what she called "a true honorable position in society" did not include the literary life at all. As late as 1845, when Browning was thirty-three and courting Elizabeth Barrett, his mother was still suggesting that he study law or medicine. Browning told Miss Barrett that they were having "many good battles" on the subject.

Meanwhile, Browning lived at home, went on with his arcane reading, and trained himself in more graces with more tutors. We do not know when he actually claimed to be regarded as a career poet. In March, 1833, his first published work, the long monologue called *Pauline*, was very coldly received; and he went back rebuffed to his friends and studies. By that time he had begun to make consular acquaintances. One of his new contacts, George de Benkhausen, the Russian consul general, added Browning to his staff for a flying trip to St. Petersburg. Browning's first journey abroad was a very strange one since they posted across Europe and the steppes without halting and posted back with the same skimming celerity. Browning was able to see something of the Russian capital, however, and conceived a little drama about a "Player-girl" and "a fair on the Neva, and booths and droshkies and fish-pies and so forth"[5]—the original trial, I think for what was to be reset in Italy and called *Pippa Passes.*

Returned to London he found a more intimate acquaintance in a young French diplomat, the Comte Amédée de Ripert-Monclar. Monclar, who was literary himself, had the additional distinction of being a secret courier between Royalist groups in France and Royalists who had fled to England after the revolution of 1830. It was Monclar who suggested the primitive chemist Paracelsus as the subject of a second long poem. That Browning was dazzled by this romantic young nobleman is clear from the gushiness of the dedication which he attached to the finished *Paracelsus,* which he published in 1835.

The desire to travel and the glamor of his new friendships made Browning consider the advantages of a diplomatic career. His good sense no doubt reminded him that the iron facts of caste and money would prevent his rising to the top in that calling. Besides, there was the poetry to which he had insisted he was devoting his life. By the publication of *Paracelsus,* in 1835, he confirmed himself as a career poet. The éclat given him by *Paracelsus* led to his being invited to write a play, and to his passionate and long-protracted efforts to write successfully for the stage. Meanwhile, he worked with steadily accelerating interest on a series of shorter poems, chiefly lyrics and monologues. For the next ten years he was to split his creative efforts into the three modular groups of book-length story-poems, full-scale dramas, and short poems. Though at the expense of some overlapping, it is useful to handle each mode separately, in the order in which each engrossed the attention of the poet.

CHAPTER 2

Nondramatic Book–Poems

Pauline *to* A Soul's Tragedy

I *Drama Discriminated*

THE great names in English poetry have tended to be thought of first as authors of long works, a *Canterbury Tales*, *Faerie Queene*, or *Paradise Lost*. Tennyson took a different course, but Browning went with the principle that a poem might as well fill a book. His early production of book-length nondramatic poems was interspersed with production of pieces meant for the stage. But a separate discussion of the two groups is called for by Browning's own view of the matter: a poem, he asserted more than once, was "not a drama"; and the test of a drama was its suitability for the stage. In the little-known preface placed before the first edition of *Paracelsus*, and subsequently dropped, he elucidated the distinction:

I have endeavored to write a poem, not a drama: the canons of drama are well known, and I cannot but think that, inasmuch as they have immediate regard to stage presentation, the peculiar advantages they hold out are really such only so long as the purpose for which they were first instituted is kept in view. I do not very well understand what is called a Dramatic Poem, wherein all those restrictions only submitted to on account of compensating good in the original scheme are scrupulously retained... and all new facilities placed at an author's disposal by the vehicle he selects, as scrupulously rejected.

Browning's only writings which had "immediate regard to stage presentation" were *Strafford*, *King Victor and King Charles*, *The Return of the Druses*, *A Blot in the 'Scutcheon*,

21

Columbe's Birthday, and *Luria.* His long poems written to the different scheme and meant to be read rather than staged are *Pauline, Paracelsus, Sordello, Pippa Passes,* and *A Soul's Tragedy*—the works discussed in this chapter.

II Pauline

Pauline, a Fragment of a Confession, terminates with the dateline "Richmond, 2nd October, 1832." Browning never lived or wrote in Richmond. What the date commemorates is his attendance at a dramatic performance by the great actor Edmund Kean, who was acting out his final years in a small theater in that suburb. At the performance, the young Browning had worked out a system of deliberate disguises for wear as he entered literature: "The following poem," he wrote in an edition of 1887, "was written in pursuit of a foolish plan which occupied me mightily for a time, and which had for its object the enabling me to assume and realize I know not how many characters: —meanwhile the world was never to guess that 'Brown, Smith, Jones, and Robinson' . . . the respective authors of this poem, the other novel, such an opera, such a speech, etc., etc., were no other than one and the same individual." Browning acknowledges that the speaker in *Pauline* "would have been more legitimately myself than most of the others," except that he had been cloudily "surrounded . . . with all manner of (to my then notion) poetical accessories."

Real or unreal, the "confession" was printed at the expense of Sarah Anna's sister, Mrs. Silverthorne, the wife of a prosperous brewer whose plant challenged the skies near Browning's house in Camberwell. No name appeared on the title page, and mystifications of other kinds are to be found throughout. The speaker, for example, claims in some places to be twenty and in others to be viewing twenty from a later period. His Pauline, the person loved by the speaker, who also hears his "confession," adds a long note in which he is analyzed from the standpoint of morbid psychology. Her analysis is written in French, though in the text she is cited as of Baltic origin:

> The land that gave thee life shall be our home,
> Where nature lies all wild amid her lakes
> And snow-swathed mountains and vast pines begirt
> With ropes of snow—where nature lies all bare,

> Suffering none to view her but a race
> Of stinted or deformed. (ll. 951-56)

In its center the poem makes a basically serious attempt to describe a descent from faith in God through a series of spheres which end in belief in the self only.

In youth, whether now or earlier, the speaker has been unusually active, intense, and self-aware. He admits "a principle of restlessness/Which would be all, have, see, know, taste, feel, all." Though unusually full, his imaginative life is well in control; this peruser of old horrors "can take a secret pride in calling/The dark past up to quell it regally." Self-torture leads to other ills:

> Long restraint chained down
> My soul till it was changed. I lost myself
> And were it not that I so loathe that loss,
> I could recall how first I learned to turn
> The mind against itself; and the effects
> In deeds for which remorse were vain as for
> The wanderings of delirious dream; yet thence
> Came cunning, envy, falsehood, all world's wrong
> That spotted me. (ll. 344-52)

Somehow he "cleansed himself" and "peace returned." He now "sings"; and his "song" is pure and natural, though imitative. Faith and love are still suspended.

After another "pause," the speaker grasps "Not so much on a system as a man"—Shelley, whom he calls "Sun-treader":

> Soon the orb
> Of his conceptions dawned on me ... I threw myself
> To meet it, I was vowed to liberty
> Men were to be as Gods and earth as heaven,
> And I—ah, what a life was mine to prove!
> My whole soul rose to meet it. (ll. 419-28)

What he has reached was the revolutionary deification of mankind. Yet this new deity will not do, and he awakes "as from a dream":

> I said, " 'Twas beautiful,
> Yet but a dream, and so adieu to it!" ...

> First went my hopes of perfecting mankind
> Next—faith in them, and then in Freedom's self
> And Virtue's self, then my own motives, ends,
> And aims and loves, and human love went last. (ll. 449-61)

In his new freedom from ideals, he experiences "new powers" such as "wit, mockery,/Light-heartedness," and casts "Hope joyously away." There follows a dramatic reverie full of spirits and personifications, adduced to show the self-analysis of the speaker after another "pause." He admits the extraordinary power which follows the remission of outside sanctions. He can act with perfect autonomy at last. But he perceives the classical defects of egocentric philosophies as well:

> I seem more warped in this than aught,
> Myself stands out more hideously: of old
> I could forget myself in friendship, fame,
> Liberty, nay in love of mightier souls;
> But I begin to know what thing hate is—
> To sicken and to quiver and grow white—
> And I myself have furnished its first prey.
> Hate of the weak and ever-wavering will,
> The selfishness and still-decaying frame. (ll. 646-54

Pauline, who has been inert so far, now joins the speaker in a long Faust-flight through a series of romantic woods and ranges. They are to go, or else have already gone, to Tibet or wherever her cold home is, and gradually establish the knowledge that "God loves us, and that all which errs/Is but a dream which death will dissipate." He can now make "an end in perfect joy"—

> As I again go o'er the tracts of thought
> Like one who has a right, and I shall live
> With poets, calmer, purer still each time,
> And beauteous shapes will come for me to seize,
> And unknown secrets will be trusted me
> Which were denied the waverer once; but now
> I shall be priest and prophet as of old. (ll. 1013-19)

"Sun-treader," he concludes, "I believe in God and truth/And love."

A résumé of this kind cannot do justice to *Pauline*. We cannot summarize effectively the wonderful ornamentation of witches and lamias, sacred insects and doomed kings, and such symbolic creations as—

> the boy
> With his white breast and brow and clustering curls
> Streaked with his mother's blood, but striving hard
> To tell his story ere his reason goes. (ll. 573-76)

Regardless of its vitality and copiousness, such a poem tends to be impaled upon the single pins of psychological analysis. A writer in *Fraser's Magazine* immediately called its author "as mad as Cassandra, without any of the power to prophesy like her, or to construct a connected sentence like anyone else." John Stuart Mill, to whom Fox passed on a copy for criticism, compared the obviously emotional poem against his own dream of a coolly rational universe and called it "morbid self-consciousness." Fox wrote a puffing review of not much interest, but Joseph Arnould made a wiser estimate a few years later when he said that *Pauline* was "a strange, wild... poet-biography... in fact, psychologically speaking, his *Sartor Resartus*."[1] Rough, roundabout, and obscure as it often is, *Pauline*, like Carlyle's *Sartor*, has a tough analytic center, a systematic construction, and much good poetry. It remains one of the best attempts by an author to convey the infection of the mind by the virus of despair.

III   Paracelsus

A long two and a half years passed between *Pauline* and Browning's next important effort, the long poem *Paracelsus*. His only other publication of the period was "Eyes calm beside me," an undistinguished sonnet, probably a salute to Eliza Flower, that was printed by Fox in his journal called *The Monthly Repository*. Some of his energies, De Vane suggests, went into trying "to forget *Pauline*";[2] for both the general neglect and the particular notice which had been accorded it had been painful to its author. By the fall of 1834, however, Browning had accepted the suggestion of his friend the Comte Amédée de Ripert-Monclar that he write a poem about Paracelsus—or, more fully, Aureole Theophrastus Bombastus van Hohenstein, who was called Paracelsus and who was a gaudy

miracle-worker, failed professor, and good pharmacist of the
early sixteenth century.

There appear to have been several stages to Browning's
concept of this poem. He may have first set out to exploit
the ethical dilemma embodied by men who do ill that good
may triumph, a dilemma which eventually became his favorite.
As a second effort, he reworked the poem so as to analyze
the effects of conflicts between emotional and intellectual
states of consciousness. He had introduced these conflicts in
Pauline:

> ... restlessness of passion meets in me
> a craving after knowledge: the sole proof
> Of yet commanding will is in that power
> Repressed; for I beheld it in its dawn,
> The sleepless harpy with just-budding wings,
> And I considered whether to forego
> All happy ignorant hopes and fears, to live,
> Finding a recompense in its wild eyes.
> And when I found that I should perish so,
> I bade its wild eyes close from me forever. (620-29)

Though the theme of *Paracelsus* can be analyzed in several
ways, this conflict between passion and reason is its heart.
Browning's choice of Paracelsus's story for his narrative vehicle
has been termed foolish or defiant. The Paracelsus of history
was of the race of Faust and Frankenstein, that is, of geniuses
so isolated by superior intellect as to become criminal or mad
or both. He had had terrible publicity, and where known at
all his history was garbled. G. K. Chesterton, who maintains
Roman Catholic attitudes throughout his spirited book on
Browning, defends the poet's choice.

It is difficult to imagine a turn of mind constituting a more complete
challenge to the ordinary modern point of view.... But for all that,
Browning was right.... In the character of Paracelsus, Browning
wished to paint the dangers and disappointments which attend the
man who believes only in the intellect. He wished to depict the
fall of the logician; and with a perfect and unerring instinct he selected
a man who wrote and spoke in the tradition of the Middle Ages,
the most thoroughly and even painfully logical period that the world
has ever seen.... It would have been hard ... for Browning to have

chosen a better example for his study of intellectual egotism than Paracelsus.[3]

In form, Browning's long poem is a set of monologues and dialogues arranged in five parts. As he explains in the preface, it is not a play but a poem. The curious headings for the five parts are "Paracelsus Aspires," "Paracelsus Attains," a mere "Paracelsus," then again "Paracelsus Aspires" and "Paracelsus Attains." The protagonist, a vibrantly intelligent, self-aware, and aggressive student, is shown abandoning the futile work of the schools in favor of an independent search for "truth." He surrenders friendship, beauty, society, honesty, and sanity in the pursuit of this abstraction. Of his two "attainments," one is partial, the other total. Early in his career he establishes a relationship with a young poet, Aprile, who teaches him that men must feel as well as think:

> . . . as the melodious wretch disburthened
> His heart, and moaned his weakness in my ear,
> I learned my own deep error; love's undoing
> Taught me the worth of love in man's estate
> And what proportion love should hold with power
> In his right constitution. (V. 852-57)

However, the dying pharmacist still "saw no good in man/To overbalance all the wear and waste/Of faculties":

> In my own heart love had not been made wise
> To trace love's faint beginnings in mankind,
> To know even hate is but a mask of love's,
> To see a good in evil, and a hope
> In ill-success; to sympathise, be proud
> Of their half-reasons, faint aspirings, dim
> Struggles for truth, their poorest fallacies,
> Their prejudice and fears and cares and doubts;
> All with a touch of nobleness, despite
> Their error, upwards tending all though weak
> Like plants in mines which never saw the sun
> But dream of him, and guess where he may be,
> And do their best to climb and get to him. (V. 872-84)

"All this I knew not, and I failed," he sums up. Browning has already made him speak of the evolutionary processes which will produce the superman whose power will lie in "knowledge... strengthened by love." In his last coherent statement, Paracelsus makes the prediction common to saviors who must die:

> If I stoop
> Into a dark tremendous sea of cloud,
> It is but for a time; I press God's lamp
> Close to my breast; its splendour soon or late
> Will pierce the gloom: I shall emerge one day.
> You understand me? (V. 989-93)

The concept of a hope in bitter conflict with both revelation and reason was to haunt Browning throughout his whole career.

Paracelsus got, in its time, quite good reviews. Its reliance on Shelley's musical use of verbal abstractions was mentioned in several journals, one of which objected that it paraded Shelley's "mysticism and vagueness" without matching his power. Reviewers who approved included Landor, Leigh Hunt, Ralph Waldo Emerson, and of course Fox. The energetic young journalist John Forster, who found the poem full of "unequivocal genius," thought that Browning might have "a brilliant career." Browning responded gratefully, and the two men began a friendship which lasted thirty years. Wordsworth, at a party, expressed himself "proud to drink your health, Mr. Browning." Thus *Paracelsus* took hold of literary people in a rather short time, and let Browning feel at home among them. The title pages of some nine of the next ten books to be published by Browning bore the legend "By the Author of *Paracelsus*" as a mark of distinction.

IV   Sordello *and Smash*

As already noticed, *Sordello* was begun in 1833 while the failure of *Pauline* was still an open wound to Browning. He had determined to cast his future studies of sensitive or creative souls in the third person so that reflections such as that of Mill would not attach to his own personality. His other set objectives in *Sordello* were to "clarify" the psychological issues raised in the earlier poem and to vindicate persons who were emotionally hard-pressed from the charge of weakness. He felt sure of the poem, took to discussing it with his friends, and advertised it through his publisher in the most pleasant kind of anticipation. Meanwhile he read, traveled, discovered Asolo—always his favorite town thereafter—and collected the details of local color and the data of siege, battle, and civic torment which make *Sordello* interesting as a panorama of medieval life. Actual history was not especially wanted, for Browning considered his whole historical framework to be a "decoration . . . of no more importance than the background requires." He wanted simplicity. His poem, he strangely thought, would be "more popular and perhaps less difficult" than either *Pauline* or *Paracelsus.*

Browning's first burst of energy produced roughly the first two and half of the six books into which the completed poem was divided. In this part, he tells a rather unified story of the "development of a soul" that culminates in a prime expressiveness in art—his own story, he thought, as well as Shelley's. The second burst of energy occurred after his completion of the political stage-play *Strafford,* and led him to add many political and military passages intended to illustrate conflicts between the life of ideals and intellect and the life of purpose and action. In July, 1837, Browning was shocked to learn that a rival poem about his hero Sordello was being published. This poem, the work of a Mrs. W. Busk, had few things in common with Browning's. Browning was sensitive and apprehensive, however, and set about making a long series of changes and enlargements.

Researches in aid of this abortive new effort included journeys in Italy and considerable additional reading. From these researches he developed a new theme; for, while "seated on a step in Venice," he became suddenly aware that the real sufferers from princely wars and politics were the common people. In a fourth shift of feeling, he developed a conflict between an altruistic social conscience exemplified by *Sordello,* and an opportunistic practical statesmanship exemplified in the soldierly character of Taurello Salinguerra, the chief warlord of Northern Italy. At some time in the process, Browning was struck by the possibility that Sordello might be a lost son of Salinguerra. Nothing like that had been suggested by any historian, but Browning had by this time lost touch with anything that might really have happened. His *Sordello* had taken on an independent life, and he was oblivious not only to what historians might have said, but also to what the readers of literature might think.

Contrary to popular legend, the plot of *Sordello* is not difficult to follow. A sensitive and solitary boy, Sordello grows up in the castle of Goito, near Mantua but isolated from it. Only after achieving full manhood and the skills of the troubadour does he reach the city. A tournament or "court of love" is just ending in song; and Sordello, after hearing a song by Eglamour, the leading troubadour of the region, "picks up the harp" and continues the song so exquisitely that he is acclaimed chief singer, and Eglamour dies broken-hearted. After his success as a musician, Sordello becomes an important citizen and soldier of the Mantuan commonwealth; and Palma, a young noblewoman with Ghibbeline connections, falls in love with him. The story disintegrates at this point; Browning, editorializing, devotes hundreds of lines to developing the idea that high, truly high, service implies service to the lowly. The "dizened... chiefs and bards" will, he says, monopolize his attentions no more.

The second half of the poem (from the beginning of Part IV) begins with a terrifyingly clear and vivid list of horrors visited upon citizens in the siege of Ferrara. Drifting through the miseries comes Sordello, guided by Palma; and there is a scene in which Sordello learns that he and Salinguerra, the general who presides over the horrors, are son and father. After this point, attention is entirely focused on Salinguerra. In a good, long scene, Salinguerra plans half whimsically, half seriously, to carve out an Italian empire for his newfound son. Sordello must now decide whether to rule his people or to serve them from their own level. Shall he be lordly Ghibbeline or more liberal Guelph? He does not decide, however, but dies from emotional stress arising from the problem. A few hundred lines are added to show how, in torture or in shame, the other principals of the story end their careers.

Browning's amalgamation of variant plans eventuated in the creation of several Sordellos and more themes, arguments, and incidents than may easily be counted. Friendly criticism may allege the orderly rise of Sordello's personality through three stages: from romantic solitary, to patriotic soldier, to altruistic social reformer with sympathies so powerful as to be fatal. No critical bias in favor of the poem could show unity or progress in the historical, philosophical, and fictional burden of the whole poem. The effect of its confusion on Browning's swiftly developing career was disastrous. Aphorisms and bon mots on Browning's pretentiousness and obscurity swept through the reading public. Several people, one an admired friend of Browning's, had read the book and shuddered lest *they* be going crazy. After a careful reading, Mrs. Carlyle said that she did not know whether "Sordello" was a city, a man, or a book. Tennyson, noting that the poem began "Who will may hear Sordello's story told," and ended "Who would, has heard Sordello's story told," remarked that these were the only two sentences he understood—and that both were lies.[4] For the rest of his life Browning was made to suffer for the creation of this nearly unreadable long poem.

V *Bells and Pomegranates, and* Pippa

That the release of *Sordello* in its original form was a catastrophic error was as obvious to Browning and his friends as to its mocking readers. From time to time for the next decade he took the book up again, thinking to improve it; but in each instance he turned away disgusted. Meanwhile, as "the author of *Sordello*" he could not get exposure for his other works. Producers would not look seriously at his plays, nor publishers at his poetry. The recourse suggested to him by the poet-publisher Edward Moxon was release of his work in a series of pamphlets printed at his own expense. This sensible and modest exposure would, as Moxon argued, help remove the implications of distractedness and arrogance which had attached to Browning through the flaunting *Sordello*. Browning's father was drawn into the scheme as financial backer, and the name "Bells and Pomegranates" (from an Old Testament allusion to the ornamentation of priest's costumes) was attached to it. Originally the series was intended to include only "a series of Dramatic Pieces . . . which . . . will . . . help me to a sort of Pit-audience again."[5] But the third and sixth of the pamphlets were collections of short poems; and *Pippa Passes*, which was wisely chosen to lead off the series, was not a play in the usual sense. Curiously, it was the nonplay pamphlets—numbers One, Three, and Six—which reestab-

lished Browning's reputation. The actual dramas, which are
treated in a subsequent chapter, are of lower quality, and did
little more than keep Browning's name before the public.

   Pippa Passes, the book-length masterpiece published as the
first pamphlet of the Bells and Pomegranates series, was conceived during a solitary walk of Browning's through Dulwich
Wood. On that occasion, as he told his friend and first biographer Mrs. Orr, "the image flashed upon him of walking alone
through life; one apparently too obscure to leave a trace of
his or her passage, yet exercising a lasting though unconscious
influence at every step of it."[6] The choice of a working-class
girl as heroine had struck him years earlier, after his Russian
journey. The persons to be influenced by little Pippa were
lawbreakers, losers, and neurotics apparently left over from
the downbeat personnel of *Sordello*. The action of *Pippa Passes*
begins just where the action of *Sordello* ended, that is, with
a barefoot child in Asolo climbing hopefully up a hillside wet
with dew, singing songs "to beat the lark, God's poet." The
previous lives of little silk-factory worker and lofty and noble
poet have been similar: both have been stolen as children
and reared by strangers; both await the discovery of their
families and their own identities. But Pippa's hopefulness,
good cheer, and realistic objectives are in contrast with the
dejection, pessimism, and brokenly philosophic thinking of
Sordello. It is almost as though Browning had deliberately
decided to maintain the same conditions while he reversed
his protagonist's attitudes.

   Pippa's charm, high spirits, and "optimism" have been
wrongly ascribed to Browning by five generations of sentimental writers. Browning's view of the cosmos is not summarized
in her little song ending, "God's in his Heaven,/All's right
with the world." Nor does the celebrated jingle even represent
Pippa's general thinking, for Pippa too can discriminate between what is wrong and what is right with the world. Her
discrimination occurs within the narrow limits of her knowledge, of course. The empathy she seeks to establish, during
the single annual holiday into which the action is crowded,
is with people whom she thinks "the happiest Four in Asolo,"
but who are in fact the most brutal, confused, neurotic, and
threatened. The four scenes through which she "passes" singing her happy songs are as scabrous as any four linked scenes
in English literature. The scenes are named for times of the

day. In "Morning," she passes the lascivious Ottima, who with her kept lover Sebald has just murdered her rich old husband. In "Noon," she passes the poor art-student Jules, who is just discovering that his pretty new bride is an experienced whore from a Roman brothel. In "Afternoon," her songs reach Luigi, a tormented young Italian patriot just setting out on a mission to kill the Austrian governor. In "Night," coming closer to her own destiny, she passes under the window of a cynical and worldly old Monsignor, who is at that moment balancing the temptation of having Pippa abducted and placed in a brothel, where, as Browning assures us, she will die of abuse and disease within three years. At stake is a secret inheritance which the Monsignor knows about but the trusting Pippa does not. The odds and ends of humanity whom Pippa meets casually "by the way" are as unlovely as those she passes in the set scenes—foul-mouthed students, agents of the secret police, quarreling young prostitutes, and above all the ineffable Bluephocks, one of Browning's finest creations, an Italianate Englishman who is comedian, madman, scholar, and devil rolled into one. Through Pippa's songs, some ameliorations or reforms in individuals occur; but her phrase "all's right" is contradicted by the persons and circumstances of the composition.

Pippa Passes was the best possible commencement of Browning's slow but determined effort at professional self-rehabilitation. Its critical reception lacked fanfare; but, quietly appreciated upon publication, it kept being recollected with favor. During their courtship, Browning and Elizabeth Barrett agreed that it was his best long composition. Miss Barrett, who exempted it from her general view about his dramatic techniques, asserted that this dramatic poem was the work of his that she would most like to number among her own writings. The sheer energy of the poem, its boldness of conception, its masterly combination of styles, its fearless progress through the proscribed and forbidden, and, above all, its swarming field of folk, make it one of the finest single pieces in English literature; and it remains the best known and most admired of all Browning's long works.

VI   A Soul's Tragedy, *and* Out

A Soul's Tragedy was written as early as 1841, shortly after the completion of *Pippa Passes*. Browning's inspiration for the new dramatic poem derived from his political studies of the time, and engrossed his mature suspicion of the whole syndrome of revolutionary thinking. Like *Pippa Passes*, this poem employs whirling Elizabethan prose to show the darker and more painful aspects of the thinking of people under stress. But the author who rightly loved his *Pippa* did not love his *Soul's Tragedy*. He kept it out of sight during the four years of his effort to write stage plays; and in 1846, when he first let it be read, he downgraded it as "all sneering and disillusion," and offered to burn it if the reader agreed. But the reader was Elizabeth Barrett. Though not suggesting that it was Browning's best work, Miss Barrett found the poem warm, vital, and colorful. "It delights me," she wrote, "and must raise your reputation as poet and thinker."[7] Browning consequently added it to *Luria*, his bad stage-play with its quite different view of politics, to complete the eighth and last pamphlet of "Bells and Pomegranates."

A Soul's Tragedy has action comprising two days, separated by a period of a week or so. Day One, called Act One in some editions, gives "the poetry of Chiappino's Life"; Day Two, or Act Two, gives "its prose." The sixteenth-century Chiappino shown in the first act is an aggressive, radical, all-or-nothing political outlaw who has agitated against a tyrannical provost of the town of Faenza. His friend Luitolfo is a moderate reformist whom people tend to love and trust. The fact that both happen to love the same girl, Eulalia, is not really important in this political antiromance; for the contrast is between the men. The extremist Chiappino has only disdain for the cheerful gradualism of Luitolfo:

> You'll play, will you?
> Diversity your tactics, give submission,
> Obsequiousness and flattery a turn,
> While we die in our misery patient deaths?
> We all are outraged then, and I the first:
> I, for mankind, resent each shrug and smirk,
> Each beck and bend, each . . . all you do and are. (ll. 108-14)

Chiappino's militant plan is to kill the governor; but the moderate Luitolfo, accidentally goaded into fury, actually does the deed. And in a grand sacrificial gesture which closes the first act, Chiappino confesses the killing as his own, while Luitolfo escapes into exile. The second act, written entirely in prose, shows Chiappino's swift descent from this moral pinnacle. Rather than being executed, he is raised to political eminence by his supposed slaughter of the governor, and from this eminence he sees everything differently. He is encouraged in his new views by Ogniben, the Pope's legate, who has already watched "three and twenty leaders of revolts" turn conservative and tyrannous after achieving power. By the end of the day covered in Act Two, the legate leaves town with the quietly cynical comment. "Now I have known *four* and twenty leaders of revolts."

This rather unpleasant thematic irony is supported by various other ironies of circumstance and speech. At the end, for example, the reformer-turned-demagogue, who is about to be made governor for his (false) killing of the former governor, learns that he will also be executed (truly) for the deed. More legitimate are the various paradoxes cast out by the talkative Ogniben, the legate. Eulalia has suggested "the trite saying that we must not trust profession, only performance":

OGNIBEN. She'll not say that, sir, when she knows you longer; you'll instruct her better. Ever judge of men by their professions. For though the bright moment of promising is but a moment and cannot be prolonged, yet, if sincere in its moment's extravagant goodness, why, trust it and know the man by it, I say—not by his performance; which is half the world's work, interfere as the world needs must, with its accidents and circumstances: the profession was purely the man's own. I judge people by what they might be,—not are, nor will be.

Chiappino's troubles are buried under such snow. Browning called *A Soul's Tragedy* "a wise metaphysical play" when it was in progress. It is among the most clean-lined and vigorous of all his long pieces, and present a most convincing, if most cynical, account of the classic phenomenon by which revolutionary reformers once in power turn reactionary and repressive.

CHAPTER 3

"Browning/ . . . Writer of Plays"

I *Onto the Stage*

B ROWNING closed his hard little poem "A Light Woman," published in 1855 (in *Men and Women*) but written years earlier, with these lines:

> . . . Robert Browning, you writer of plays,
> Here's a subject made to your hand.

The lines express Browning's main career objective for a full decade. They insist upon his identity as a playwright; and suggest desire to transcend the actualities of his professional performance, for "A Light Woman" presents a sophisticated modern possibility of much more intrinsic interest than the melodramatic themes he was actually using in plays. They also suggest, unfortunately, Browning's idea that a sharp twist or paradox, what we might now call a gimmick, would fit a "subject" to the hand of a playwright. "A Light Woman" is mostly paradox. An ambitious coquette, the "light woman," aims to add "my friend" to the scores or hundreds of men she has caused to fall in love with her. The "I" extricates his friend by making the woman fall in love, utterly and honestly, with himself. But now not one of them is happy:

> . . . I, what I seem to my friend, you see—
> What I soon shall seem to his love, you guess.
> What I seem to myself, do you ask of me?
> No hero, I confess. . . .
>
> One likes to show the truth for the truth;
> That the woman was light is very true:
> But suppose she says,—never mind that youth—
> What wrong have I done to you?

The paradox and piquancy which attach to the situation might indeed embellish a play. Compared to basic elements such as characterization, conflict, scene-structure, and the parabolic strategies of high drama, they would be unimportant—a fact that Browning in his role as playwright was never to learn.

His opportunity to assume the role had come, paradoxically, through his writing of *Paracelsus* in a straight line, with scarcely a hint of the situational contretemps which were to delight him—and fatally hamper him—during his decade as a "writer of plays." Though pronounced "not for acting" by its author, *Paracelsus* had attracted the attention of William Charles Macready, the leading figure in Drury Lane and a presiding actor-manager of his time. At Macready's instigation, Browning, in the late summer of 1836, commenced work on his first play. There was some sparring with a Roman subject, the life of Narses; but the subject finally chosen was the life of another historical character, the seventeenth-century royalist Strafford. Though begun in a spirit of mutual esteem, *Strafford* led to a considerable suspicion and dislike between author and the actor-manager. Macready's faithfully kept diaries provide a fascinating record of the excitement, stress, and egotism which at that time marked Browning's character. But, after much patching and repairing, and after many quarrels not only with Macready but with the actress Helen Faucit and other theatrical personages, and with his friends Forster and Fox, Browning witnessed his debut as a dramatist at Drury Lane.

II Strafford

Strafford, an historical play, follows the conventions of Elizabethan plays of the same genre. The subject had come to Browning's hand through assistance which he had given to Forster in the writing of a biography of Thomas Wentworth, Earl of Strafford, an unlucky soldier and statesman in service of the unlucky Charles I. What Browning half found and half created in the life of Strafford was stressful paradox. The Strafford proposed by Browning is that classic type of loser who loses not because he is worse than men around him but because he is better. His political career is shown to be climaxing in 1639-41 when the conflict between Charles I and the House of Commons was just turning fatal and when Strafford had shifted from a stern loyalty to the Commons to an equally

stern loyalty to the King. Browning presents his hero as energetic, self-sacrificing, and faithful to Charles because of personal affection as well as Royalist principles. But his old
associates naturally regard him as a turncoat, and the King
is too stupid and weak to support him. Strafford's growing
agonies are principally machinated by the Puritan politician
William Pym, who is presented as his old friend now turned
fanatical enemy; and by the beautiful Countess of Carlyle,
a rather ambiguous lady, half lover and half politician, who
keeps warning him of his dangers and at one point musters
a private military force intended to support him. Of course,
nothing works. Attacked by the King's open enemies, harassed
by the King's bad friends, and left unprotected by the King
himself, Strafford is doomed for the headman's axe.

Macready's verdict that *Strafford* had "truth of character"
but also "meanness of plot, and occasional obscurity"[1] is
perhaps fair enough. The concept of the tragic protagonist
is quite successful, for what Browning intended to project was
that destructive solitude may come to a man as an ironic result
of his extraordinary capacity to love and serve. This paradox
of the lofty man who falls because of his loftiness was to appear
in all of Browning's plays and much of his other writing. But
the concept alone is not enough to save the play of *Strafford*.
Its plot is strained, its scenes rigid and static, and its language
marred by the broken syntax and skewed semantics that were
soon to madden readers of *Sordello*.

III   King Victor and King Charles

As we indicated in Chapter Two, Browning's attempt to
rehabilitate himself after *Sordello* took the form of the
pamphlet series "Bells and Pomegranates." His second play
intended for the stage, *King Victor and King Charles*, was
published in 1842 as the second pamphlet of the series. In
1839 he had offered it to Macready, who quickly judged it
"a great mistake" and "called Browning into my room and
explicitly told him so, and gave him my reasons."[2] As a closet
drama, for reading only, *King Victor and King Charles* would
also need to be regarded as a mistake. Critics have not praised
it, and it is not read.

Its data from actual history are recondite and un-British.

Victor, an eighteenth-century King of Sardinia, had put together his rather large kingdom on the Italian mainland by sheer ambition and talent. Near the end of his life, having endeared himself to his subjects by vastly improving their arts, sciences, and social arrangements, he took the unexpected step of abdicating the throne in favor of his son Charles. Charles had been unpromising as a prince and was not, in Victor's judgment, much better as a king. Within a year, senile, apoplectic, and swiftly declining, but driven forward by an ambitious new wife, the father was seeking his own reinstatement as king. However, their ruinous ex-hero was no longer acceptable to the leading spirits of the kingdom; and Victor was hustled away to die quietly in genteel imprisonment. Charles, now left with the throne, let Sardinia drift towards ignominy and extinction. History presents him as a melancholy, vacillating, spiritless creature, the precise opposite of his energetic father.

Browning's treatment of these unusual events is simple in form though not in content. The play has only four speaking parts: the two kings, Victor and Charles; the young wife of Charles; and the neutral D'Ormeo who serves both kings as the prime minister. The play has two acts somewhat divided in time. In the first, old Victor, though just then abandoning his crown, is the tough central figure. In the second, which shows King Victor's attempt to repossess the crown, King Charles's anxieties and hysterias are to the fore. An exchange of messily sentimental posturings at the conclusion produces offsetting triumphs of the spirit for both men. Browning's Lear and his Richard III, his worn ancient, and weak stripling, simply cancel each other.

Browning's unwillingness to select either Charles or Victor for a protagonist is easily related to his own personal division between the romantic and the realist, the dreamer and the aggressive salesman, the qualities we recklessly call "feminine" and "masculine." In *Strafford*, following lines of history not so easy to tamper with, he had been forced to elect the vital and determined man, rather than the drifting and uncertain one, as his protagonist. The dim politics of an *ad hoc* empire like Sardinia was not so restrictive; and he used his freedom not so much to isolate a psychological integer as to keep from isolating one. This fatal process, the direct reverse of processes used by Shakespeare, renders *King Victor and King Charles* as fallacious as art as it is as history.

IV   *The Return of the Druses*

The limpness of *King Victor and King Charles* was apparently recognized by Browning. Writing to Fanny Haworth while the play was still in progress, he explained his desire to "contrast" against it "a subject of the most wild and passionate love." His mind, he said, was full of "half-concepts, floating fancies" about such a play.[3] Contemporary attention was being drawn to the Druse nation and its religion by political turbulence in the Middle East and Browning's concepts and fancies attached themselves to the Druses of earlier history. From these semi-Arab people he drew, however, only social and religious ideas; in his plotting, he forsook history entirely and, for the first time, tried his hand at invention.

As a result, Browning introduces not the Druses generally but an offshoot tribe that has established itself on an island in the Mediterranean and gradually been enslaved by the order of Knights Hospitalers. In the year "14—," young Djabel, a tribesman educated in Europe, returns with the purpose of freeing his people and reestablishing them in Lebanon. He takes appropriate political steps and arranges for a Venetian fleet to do the job of repatriation. The main element of his plan, however, is his revitalizing of the flaccid and brutalized people by pretending to be the man whom their religion has marked for the reincarnation of God. Cheating them to serve them, he will be their divinity as well as their leader. In the single day of the dramatic action, friends, enemies, and the transport fleet converge upon the island; and accidents and misunderstandings of every sort spoil Djabel's plans. Not only his foes (a cynical Hospitaler governor and a venal Bishop-Nuncio) but his admirers (a passionately loyal Druse maiden and a young French knight) misconstrue and distrust his program. The ethical confusions produced by his double standing as a patriot and as a liar, as a true man and a false god, place him in contradictory relationships with every other person. Specious ironies of plot and circumstance sprout like mushrooms in this soil, and the characters are forced into the most hysterical shifts of posture and emotion.

Not only did Macready refuse to stage the play, but he

deduced from it that Browning was losing his mind. Browning's disappointment drove him to silly and tendentious defenses of the play—to "self-opinionated persuasions," as Macready called them in his diary. Rejected once and for all, the manuscript lay unused for two and a half years. Finding advantage in a bloody new war involving the Druses, Browning published it as the fourth number of "Bells and Pomegranates." Its faults as closet drama include the sentimentality, posturing, and bewildering complexity of motive and action. But interest is maintained by the vigorous flow of encounters, and a modern producer would not fail to notice the technicolor splendors of the half-dozen good mob-scenes. Moreover, especially in speeches by the worldly old governor and the corrupt old bishop, we hear the cadence of Browning's matured blank verse. The governor, indeed, leads the whole mighty parade of philosophical rapscallions who were to come from Browning's pen. The action of the pure knight Loys has deprived this sensual governor of the delights of rape and robbery, but he assures Loys that a favor has been done him:

> With this alcove's delicious memories
> Began to mingle visions of gaunt fathers,
> Quick-eyed sons, fugitives from the mine, the oar,
> Stealing to catch me. Brief, when I began
> To quake with fear. . . .
>   I say,
> Just when, for the remainder of my life
> All methods of escape seemed lost—just then
> Up should a young hot-headed Loys spring,
> Talk very long and loud,—in fine, compel
> The Knights to break their whole arrangement, have me
> Home for pure shame—from this safehold of mine
> Where but ten thousand Druses seek my life,
> To my wild place of banishment, San Gines
> By Murcia, where my three fat manors lying,
> Purchased by gains here and the Nuncio's gold
> Are all I have to guard me—that such fortune
> Should fall to me, I hardly could expect.
> Therefore I say, I love you. (257-76)

The final important departure of *The Return of the Druses* is its emphasis on disguise and imposture. Not a good play,

it served to instruct its author about a number of literary oppor-
tunities he had not noticed before and foreshadowed much
of the best of the work he was to do.

V   A Blot in the 'Scutcheon

Late in 1840 Browning sent Macready a play which, he
urged, was full of *"action* ... drabbing, stabbing, et autres
gentillesses."[4] Macready's own life and career at the time were
also full of trouble, and he left the play unassessed for one
year and unplayed for two. But Charles Dickens prompted
him to action; for, when asked by Forster to read the play
and give an opinion, Dickens exploded into praise. *A Blot
in the 'Scutcheon* was "lovely, true, deeply affecting"; and
it was "full of genius, natural and great thoughts, profound
and yet simple and beautiful in its vigour." He judged it "a
tragedy that *must* be played, and must be played, moreover,
by Macready."[5] Macready was still doubtful; and by February
11, 1843, when the play reached the boards, a dozen incidents
of jealousy and distrust had separated manager from writer.
Browning's pique expressed itself in his hasty printing of the
play as the fifth pamphlet of "Bells and Pomegranates" and
by his causing it to be sold at the theater on opening night.
Playgoers, he thought, should have a chance to see how a
good play was being ruined by Macready and the actors.

In theme, *A Blot* is similar to *Romeo and Juliet.* Its principal
characters are five in number—Lord Tresham, the cynosure
of the peerage, a man too fond of contemplating family honor;
Mildred Tresham, his fourteen-year-old sister; Mertoun, an
adolescent Earl from a neighboring estate; and Austin and
Guendolyn Tresham, a married pair whose witty and realistic
views of life are borrowed from the Benedick and Beatrice
of Shakespeare's *Much Ado About Nothing.* The great Tresham
countryhouse is the setting, and the action covers only two
days.

Early scenes of *A Blot* show Lord Tresham at the work of
preparing for the betrothal of Mildred and Mertoun. Ensuing
scenes develop the uncomfortable fact that the engaged children have been lovers, and carnal ones, for a long time already.
After some twenty couplings by the balcony route alone, they
have begun to sense, however, their guilt; and the betrothal
that is being celebrated as the play opens has been their intel-

ligent solution to the difficulty. But Tresham's discovery that his little sister is unchaste leads to hysterical ravings; and his discovery that the stealthy fornicator and the bright groom-to-be are one single person leads to a duel under yew-trees and to a series of death scenes in which each victim speaks, to forgive and be forgiven, before he dies. Spitted upon Tresham's rapier, young Mertoun forgives him. Her life evaporating from sheer overstress of emotions, Mildred forgives Tresham. Self-poisoned and dying in agony, Lord Tresham rather confusingly appears to be forgiving himself since he argues that "Blood/Must wash the blot away. The first blot came/And then the blood came." In the final line, the clear-eyed Guendolyn says, "Thorold, we can but—remember you," thereby raising the possibility that in Browning's view we need not necessarily share in the general exculpation.

Placed beside Shakespeare's play which it deliberately imitated, Browning's play sinks into futility. Romeo and Juliet were destroyed by the viciousness of their world as it is expressed in the emnity between their two families. But Mildred and Mertoun experienced no viciousness: their marriage is desired by everybody, and blocked only by a series of accidents. However, its well-mixed blend of pain, prurience, and gaudy emotionalism has kept *A Blot* in the eyes of readers. The passage which excited Dickens most was Mildred's analysis of her own crime:

> I was so young, I loved him so, I had
> No mother, God forgot me, and I fell.

She chimes the analysis again later, and we learn that she has uttered it nightly for the twenty or more nights of love, thinking it a prayer or charm likely to get God back on her side. Ability to take these two lines seriously is, perhaps, the key to our ability to take the whole play seriously.

VI Columbe's Birthday

Since no more could be done with the aid of Macready, Browning shifted his attention to actor-manager Charles Kean and his wife, the well-known Ellen Tree. For them, he wrote *Columbe's Birthday,* his fourth stage-play. The Keans liked the play, as Browning reported to his friends; but they were overcommitted and wished him to wait a year for the staging. Declaring that he had promised them "the stage rights only," Browning published his work as the sixth number of "Bells and Pomegranates." He had begun his two-year courtship of Elizabeth Barrett, and did not press the matter of production with the Keans or any other producer. In 1853, after the two poets had become famous expatriates, Helen Faucit wrote offering to play Columbe herself; and her elegant production ran for seven nights at the Haymarket Theater, and afterwards toured the provincial cities and America.

Columbe's Birthday has a rather clear line of action compressed, like *Pippa Passes*, into the morning-noon-afternoon-evening-night system of five acts. In the play, Columbe has been called from obscurity to become the ruler of the Duchy of Juillers and Clèves. Now, after one year of service, and on her birthday, she learns that the true monarch, Prince Berthold, is about to arrive and assume the control of the duchy. Her Juillers courtiers and citizens desert her "by instinct" even before the news is released. Into her court on the same day, however, comes one Valance, a man "never handsome and no longer young," a commoner of the neglected city of Clèves. Valance, a talkative lawyer who is called "orator" by scoffers, has been sent by the people of his city to ask relief from the high taxes and tariffs which have rendered the city desperate. He is an outspoken, no-nonsense, utterly unromantic type of man. Prince Berthold is a bold, honest, fair-minded man who is certain to rise to the throne of the Holy Roman Empire and can therefore make Columbe "the world's first woman." However, he cannot say that he passionately adores her. Valance, who has nothing to offer, can and does say that. The reader may guess Columbe's choice. In this play about chief executives, politics are contemptible and politicians are farcical. The values of the play are personal, and its sentiments are romantic. Its world is the world of musical comedy.

A play of this sort must elicit very disparate judgments. Thus Elizabeth Barrett, who had liked the play when she read it, resigned herself to believe that its week of public favor was mere "*succès d'estime.*" She wrote: "There could be no 'run' for a play of this kind," and she blamed the tastes of theater audiences. Forster, reading the play in its pamphlet form,

found it "abominable" in motive and taste—and thereby for-
feited Browning's friendship for years. A reviewer in the
Athenaeum, in 1853, experienced "often . . . the involuntary
tear . . . upon the cheek,"[6] but we cannot easily see why.

The modern reader will find in *Columbe's Birthday* a full
share of the energetic scenes and steady forward progress
needed in such a play. We quite like Columbe, Berthold, and
Valance, especially when they are being stubborn and intran-
sigent, and cannot but be amused by the gaggle of faithless
courtiers who sweep cackling from side to side as the day
progresses. The major fault of the play is not bad writing or
weak stagecraft, but a too greedy use of skewed and contradictory values. For example, ludicrous improbabilities of plot and
situation lead into perfectly straight-faced discourses on fidelity, honor, or love. Again, the politics of Clèves is presented
as grimly serious, what with its economy wrecked and its
people starving, while that of Juillers is presented only through
the farcical scrambling of tenth-rate politicians. The ability
to carry two lines side by side, one of them romantic and
the other comic, was never mastered by Browning.

VII Luria

Browning was by this time losing confidence in himself as
a playwright. His correspondence of the time is full of hints
that he will turn his energies in other directions; and he was
prepared to admit that his last two efforts, *Luria* and *A Soul's
Tragedy*, were "*manqué* . . . failures." We can follow the
development of these two writings through his correspondence
with Elizabeth Barrett. He tells about the genesis of *Luria*,
explains the motivations of its characters, and makes a rather
half-hearted defence of weaknesses which she shrewdly points
out to him. For not even Elizabeth found it in her heart to
admire this sixth and last of his attempts to write stage plays.

Luria is economical in its characters and form. Its Renaissance background and the superficial likeness of its hero to
Othello have caused most critics to compare it with
Elizabethan plays. However, it is more indebted to Greek
than to Elizabethan models. The unities of time, place, and
action are zealously adhered to; there is no onstage action;
and the emphasis is firmly placed on the Greek values of stagecraft, solitude, and irony. In the plot, which is minimal, a Moor-

ish professional soldier, Luria, has led the Florentine army
to many victories against a coalition headed by the Pisans.
He lacks sophistication in the civil arts, however, and has
come to adore Florence which he considers the queen city
in these matters. He himself is adored by his officers and sol-
diers, and lacks only one final victory over the Pisans to become
the darling of the population at large.

As the one day of the play begins, Luria is prepared to
achieve this final victory. As the day proceeds, however,
several increments of news and argument show him that the
city fathers are engaged in a secret trial designed to convict
him of misconduct and treason. Their purpose, one which in
his Othello-like innocence he cannot comprehend, is to keep
him from growing inconveniently popular among the people.
Ironic dilemma suddenly engulfs the honest soldier: shall he
turn the Florentine army around and humiliate Florence; or
shall he sit still, accept the sophisticated injustice, and let
Florence humiliate him? But he can do neither; he loves Florence and can neither demean her nor let her demean herself.
And so, at the end of the fourth act, he takes a slow poison.

In the fifth act, as Luria waits for his death, the persons
who have betrayed him rally around him again; and the city
accepts him as its savior and hero—a gratuitous new irony
which weakens rather than supports the theme. For the theme
until that time is the necessary collision of the needs of great
men with the needs of the state. The most interesting speeches
of the play, perhaps, are those in which the corrupt "statist"
Braccio explains why a government must destroy the aspirations of its finest citizens:

  ... Florence is no simple John or James
  To have his toy, his fancy, his conceit
  That he's the one excepted man by fate,
  And when fate shows him he's mistaken there,
  Die with all good men's praise, and yield his place
  To Paul and George intent to try their chance!
  Florence exists because these pass away.
  She's a contrivance to supply a type
  Of man, which man's deficiencies refuse;
  She binds so many, that she grows out of them—
  Stands steady o'er their numbers, though they change

And pass away—there s always what upholds,
Always enough to fashion the great show. (III, 177-89)

Florence has, Braccio insists, a genuine responsibility to reject and ruin her most virtuous citizens. This politics is sharply countered by the view that the viable state must model itself upon these very citizens:

> A people is but the attempt of many
> To rise to the completer life of one;
> And those who live as models for the mass
> Are singly of more value than they all....
> Such man are you, and such a time is this
> That your sole fate concerns a nation more
> Than much apparent welfare. (V, 299-304)

These lines are spoken to Luria by his enemy brother-in-arms, the Pisan Leader Tiburzio, but each of the other characters has much to say about the subject. The conflict between opposing views of the state is, indeed, the most steadily dramatic of the conflicts in the play. In this feature, along with others which have been mentioned, the play is very Grecian. Judged by the reflective standards of Greek drama, *Luria* is a reasonably substantial play. It would have staged badly, however, and Browning did not press it upon producers. Nor did he ever write another play intended for acting.

CHAPTER 4

The Short Works Called Dramatic

I *"Dramatic" as Lyric and Romance*

THE third and sixth of the pamphlets in the "Bells and Pomegranates" series bore the unit-titles *Dramatic Lyrics* and *Dramatic Romances and Lyrics*. The first contained some sixteen generally short poems, the second twenty-two. Their titles were affected by the proclaimed intent of the series to present "dramatic pieces." In a sort of double disclaimer prefacing the first collection, Browning suggested that the poems, "though for the most part Lyric in expression," were "always Dramatic in principle." Whatever was said was "so many utterances of so many imaginary persons, not mine."[1] He was, in other words, to be exculpated for his turning away from actual drama and, at the same time, exculpated for saying anything which might not prove acceptable to readers. The lessons taught him by *Pauline* and *Sordello* had made a very deep impression.

The poems of the two pamphlets were, in any case, a lively mixture of songs, lyric poems, narratives, and dialogues, capped with several masterly examples of the dramatic monologue. Some were arranged in quite arbitrary pairs and groups with fanciful titles. "Italy and France," for example, was placed as a heading over "My Last Duchess" and "Count Gismond"; "Madhouse Cells" was the heading for "Porphyria's Lover" and "Johannes Agricolae"; but most of these combining titles were afterwards dropped. In 1863, when arranging his poems for the large collective edition of that year, Browning also rearranged the poems in order to place them in what he thought to be harmonious relationships with each other and with the poems of *Men and Women* (1855). Such second thoughts—some clearly for the better, but others not—may be traced in *Robert Browning, A Bibliography*

1830–1950, compiled by L. N. Broughton, C. S. Northup, and R. B. Pearsall, and in several of the standard handbooks.

That the readers and reviewers were willing to forget *Sordello* and some of the bad dramas is established by the open-minded and generally favorable reception accorded to the two pamphlets. Then, and always afterwards, certain of the individual poems were welcomed as evidence of a fresh and original genius. The *Morning Herald,* for example, noted "the strongly original tone and . . . vivid vein of imaginativeness" of *Dramatic Lyrics;* and the *Spectator,* which had said of *King Victor and King Charles* that "Mr. Browning . . . rather cultivates his weeds than his flowers," reversed itself to call *Dramatic Lyrics* "the most readable and intelligible of all his works," to note its freedom from his usual "affectation and obscurity," and to commend "a vigour and spirit which show him capable of still better things."[2] Upon the publication of *Dramatic Romances and Lyrics* three years later, some serious critics began to accept Browning as one of the permanent British poets. This early reputation, in other words, had come to center in the thirty-eight little poems of the two little pamphlets of 1842 and 1845.

II *Circle of the Violent*

The labeling of his poems as "dramatic" was supposed to conceal the views of Browning, but the poet's tastes were not so easily concealed. In the early long poems, and in most of the plays, he had focused much loving attention on spiritual and physical agonies. His taste for violence is just as evident in the early short poems.

Virtually everyone who learns to read English is required to look at the murder poems "My Last Duchess" and "Porphyria's Lover." In "My Last Duchess," the narrator soberly explains that an incompatibility between his young wife's outgoing and affectionate character and the husband's belief in elegant personal perfection has been a proper cause for murder. The late Duchess has not discriminated; the elegant Duke discriminates absolutely. She "liked what e'er/She looked on, and her looks went everywhere." Her death proceeded from the generous breadth of her enjoyments rather than any wrongdoing:

> Who'd stoop to blame
> This sort of trifling? . . .
>   And if she let
> Herself be lessoned so, nor plainly set
> Her wits to mine, forsooth, and made excuse,
> —E'en then would be some stooping, and I choose
> Never to stoop.

Browning in his old age was encouraged by bad readers to agree that the Duke might have stopped "all smiles . . . together" by hiding his smiling wife in a nunnery; but the Duke's character, as delineated in the poem, permits no half-solution. The other famous murder, that of Porphyria, is perpetrated for the lady's well-being rather than for the man's. Porphyria's lover knows that she is frail and impure, so much so indeed that she cannot be expected to leave her wealthy husband and "give herself to me forever." But there comes a single moment of a single assignation when, as the lover sharply realizes, "Porphyria worshipped me":

> I debated what to do.
> That moment she was mine, mine, fair,
> Perfectly pure and good.

He thought of "a thing to do . . ./And strangled her," thereby achieving a permanent preservation of her otherwise momentary perfection.

Two homicidal poems of a more rough-and-tumble nature are "The Confessional" and "The Laboratory." In each a woman rather than a man tells the story. In "The Confessional," which is told as past-tense narrative, a girl in an Inquisition torture cell curses "their Priests, their Pope/Their Saints," and tells a story of fleshly fidelity and churchly treason:

> I had a lover—shame avaunt!
> This poor wrenched body, grim and gaunt,
> Was kissed all over till it burned
> By lips the truest.

Her sweet seducer has also been a liberal reformer who "schemes, men say/To change the laws of church and state." Her confessor, after hearing of her fall, suggests that she continue with the affair, learn her lover's secrets "as he lies upon my breast," and report to him what she learns so that the clergy may pray him into a holier kind of life. But her confidence is betrayed by the priest; her lover is caught and garroted; and she is tortured, locked up, and left to scream her life away with the curses for her betrayers.

"The Laboratory" is more a study than a tale. A young girl frustrated in love sits watching an old apothecary mix her a "delicate droplet" of poison. Her intended victim is a magnificent "she" who is even then trysting with the man the girl professes to love. Our speaker lusts to give pain as well as death: "Brand, burn up, bite into.../... her dying face." Besides the enemy "she," our girl hysterically dreams of killing an unidentified "Pauline," an "Elise" whose fine breast she envies, and perhaps the whole Court:

> What a wild crowd of invisible pleasures!
> To carry pure death in an earring, a casket,
> A signet, a fan-mount, a filigree basket!

Whether or not her megalomania bears fruit we are not told, but we have been told clearly that she is mad, and how, and why.

III *Six Incidents of Action*

Besides the poems which concentrate on the lethal ambitions of wrecked minds, Browning versified a number of quite simple anecdotes, the keynote of which is determined action. A suitable archetype is the "Incident of the French Camp" in which a child lieutenant reproves Napoleon, who says that he is wounded, by correctly remarking, as he falls, that he is "Not wounded sire, but killed." The other five or more of the best known action-tales are "Count Gismond," "In a Gondola," "The Flight of the Duchess," and in quite different tones, "The Glove" and "The Pied Piper."

"Count Gismond" is written in stanzas; but in its background, its chief incident, and its whirling syntax, it suggests the bloodier passages of *Sordello*. The speaker is a girl who, just as she is to be crowned Queen in a medieval Tournament of Love, is denounced as unchaste by a villainous Count Gauthier. He asks: "Shall she whose body I embraced/A night

long, queen it in the day?" Of course, she is chaste to a fault;
moreover, she is orphaned, slight of stature, and oppressed
by large and envious cousins—a pat object of our compassion.
Her deliverer is Count Gismond, who steps out of the crowd
of knights, slaughters the recreant Gauthier, and carries the
wronged virgin off to be his bride. "The Glove" is supposed
to be uttered by the Renaissance poet Peter Ronsard, and is
written in a cranky and elided style which foreshadows the
willfulness of Browning's later blank verse. In the historical
incident, which had already been handled straightforwardly
by Leigh Hunt, King Francis and his court are "watching his
lions fight" when the mistress of a peer named De Lorge tests
her lover's love by dropping her glove into the lion-pit. After
De Lorge had bravely retrieved it, he "threw the glove, but
not with love, right in the lady's face." And the king approv-
ingly comments that "Not love, you see, but jealousy/Would
set a price like that." Browning lets Ronsard develop an opposing verdict. Suppose that the lady has been testing the scarce
item love, rather than the cheap item courage? Did not De
Lorge flunk that test? In the sequel, we learn that the lady
marries well and lives happily, while De Lorge marries a frisky
adulteress and lives in cuckoldry and humiliation.

     "In a Gondola" and "The Flight of the Duchess" are tales
of female infidelity of which we are asked to approve. "In
a Gondola" takes the form of a lyric dialogue between two
lovers at the end of a tryst. Some of the dialogue is by songs,
some by "musing," and some by direct dialogue. All of it is
imbued with sexuality and Venetian local color. The lady's
husband, one of a grisly clan called "the Three," acts rather
than speaks; and, as the love-freighted gondola touches its
jetty, her lover is "surprised, and stabbed." The deeply passionate lyricism of the poem has called forth scores or hundreds
of musical settings. "The Flight of the Duchess," another runaway poem, was an instant favorite with Elizabeth Barrett; and
it is pleasant to conjecture that it helped to convince her of
the necessity of her own flight. The speaker of the poem is
a yeomanlike, rough-hewn, bluff retainer of the weakly romantic Duke and his passionate but frustrated young Duchess.
This Duke's duchy is vast and rich, but northern and cold;
and the Duke has been "told in Paris" that its genius was
medieval:

> Our rough North land was the Land of Lays
> The one good thing left in evil days
> Since the Mid-Age was the Heroic Time,
> And only in wild nooks like ours
> Could you taste of it yet as in its prime. (104–08)

Believing this theory, the Duke has turned antiquary and tried to establish ancient folkways and mores among his people, whom he likes to call "serfs and thralls." His wife, another small-bodied, great-hearted woman, finds life with this Miniver Cheevy difficult enough even when he does not insist that she help him reconstruct antiquity. On a fatal day the Duke reads that old-time noblewomen presided at the disemboweling of slain deer. The Duchess's refusal to do so draws anger and vituperation from him and his "yellow mother." But the blind, dirty, mean old gypsy crone who is sent to punish her turns out to be a Romany Queen. Under her tutelage, the Duchess learns that gypsy life offers the truth and freedom which she is not enjoying with her ever-pretending Duke, and she leaves the castle and rides off to be a gypsy. The bumbling, roundabout, humorous speech of Browning's narrator extends this simple plot to nearly a thousand lines of extraordinary vigor and originality.

The still lighter "Pied Piper of Hamelin," which Browning subtitled "A Child's Story," employs the same copia and daring. The rats are drowned, all but one who "stout as Julius Caesar" swam over and "lived to carry/ . . . /To Rat-land home his Commentary,"

> Which was, "At the first shrill notes of the pipe,
> I heard a sound as of scraping tripe,
> And putting apples, wondrous ripe,
> Into a cider-press's gripe:
> And a moving away of pickle-tub boards
> And a leaving ajar of conserve-cupboards,
> And a drawing of corks of train-oil flasks,
> And a breaking of hoops of butter-casks:
> And it seemed as if a voice
> (Sweeter far than by harp or by psaltery
> Is breathed) called out, 'Oh rats, rejoice!
> The world is grown to one vast drysaltery.' "

And so on, with an unending flood of good-humored vigor.

Verse so robust and yet so charming had literally never been
written before.

IV *Places and Periods*

Many of the poems of *Dramatic Lyrics* and *Dramatic
Romances and Lyrics* are extended lyrical allusions to geo-
graphical or historical facts which had, reasonably or un-
reasonably, attracted the attention of Browning. Any close look
at the poems will reveal factual errors. For example, the two
studies of equestrian motion, "How They Brought the Good
News" and "Through the Metidja," contain the grossest diver-
gences from possibility. The poems are, moreover, wildly disparate in mood, form, and style. But Browning relied on mem-
ory and inspiration rather than on research. Loose groupings
by subject might produce the categories of Places and Periods
—which widely overlap, however.

Browning's denial of personal involvement in poetic statements does not stretch to cover his four early lyrics on England
and Italy. Two of these, "Home Thoughts from Abroad" and
"Home Thoughts from the Sea," are justly held among the
national treasures of Britain. Many an eye which has never
seen England has danced among the beauties of "En-
gland/Now that April's there." "Home Thoughts from the Sea"
is more significant in the context of patriotic yearnings. It had
been at Cape St. Vincent and Cape Trafalgar that Lord Nelson,
whom Tennyson rightly called "the greatest sailor since the
world began," won for England her control of all the saltwater
seas. Nelson's words at the beginning and end of the Trafalgar
battle—that is, "England expects every man to do his duty,"
and, as he lay dying in his flagship, "Thank God I have done
my duty"—are handsomely echoed in Browning's lines of self-
dedication:

"Here and here has England helped me: how can I help
                              England?"—say
Whoso turns as I, this evening, turn to God to praise and pray,
While Jove's planet rises yonder, silent over Africa.

The less famous "Englishman in Italy," originally called
"England in Italy," is a long list of sights and sounds available
to a sojourner or stroller. The first half presents the how and

what of Italian foods; the second half is more discursive, but still chiefly a list. The poem is perhaps too long; it is all background, and lacks the plot or personality which would sustain its length. "The Italian in England," or originally "Italy in England," is political and romantic. An Italian patriot has escaped to England with the aid of a country girl. In his exile, he dreams of three triumphant acts: he would be at home with the girl; he would see King Charles ("perjured traitor") lying dead; he would "grasp Metternich until/I felt his wet red throat distil/In blood through these two hands."

"Waring," a poem written as a salute to Alfred Domett, Browning's best friend in the old suburban "Set," takes one cruising over the world of British-controlled salt water. Waring, proud, ambitious, and tired of his island, had "paced this London/With no work done, but great works undone." The home part is studded with interesting notes on London subliterary life. In the overseas part, Browning envisages his friend in India, in Moscow, in Greece, in the Crimea ("Scythian strands"), in Spain, and then, secretly, in Britain again. The best-drawn encounter shows him in a piratical little lugger off Trieste. But he is finally taken to be in "Vishnu-land." The original, Domett, was in New Zealand. Browning did not know it or intend it, but "Waring," better than any of his poems, suggests the apogee of Victorian Britain as the prime nation of the globe.

Just as Browning rifled the regions of the world, so did he voraciously rifle its legends and its history. "Artemis Prologizes" was by intention the summarizing first speech of a tragedy in the Greek form. Its rhythmical boldness and beauty were admired by so deliberate a classicist as Matthew Arnold:

> I am a goddess of the ambrosial courts
> And, save by Herè, Queen of Pride, surpassed
> By none whose temples whiten this the world.

The pride of Artemis shows more clearly than that of her rival, the queen-goddess, whom most people call Hera. Browning's use of "Herè" for Hera illustrates a lifetime campaign of his own to get Greek names translated in phonetic rather than traditional ways. The play, which would have been a sequel to the *Hyppolytus* of Euripides, was never written. "The Boy and the Angel" is a rather confusing little anecdote, medieval in its contents, Renaissance in its reference to "Peter's Dome," and nineteenth-century in its sentimental insistence that a poor boy's praise of God is more loved than the praise of a Pope might be.

Two poems linked under the joining title "Queen-Worship" in *Dramatic Lyrics* celebrate the unrequited love of commoners for queens; but in other ways they are quite different. One, "Rudel to the Lady of Tripoli," features the twelfth-century troubadour Rudel, who in pretty lyrics presents himself as a flower and his royal inamorata as a mountain which will not be moved. The second, "Cristina," employs Browning's own contemporary, Queen Maria Cristina of Spain, a lady famous during the middle of the century for stylishness, political energy, and the coquetry with which she attached men to her various causes. The speaker in the poem has been lured into loving her, and then been casually forgotten. Her love was only light and transient; his was (and always will be) profound and precious. He is able to explain this fidelity as a triumph for himself.

> She has lost me, I have gained her;
> Her soul's mine: and thus, grown perfect,
> I shall pass my life's remainder.

The same concept appears in "The Lost Mistress," and would later appear in "The Last Ride Together" and other poems ungrounded in history or politics.

The politics of England in the time of Lord Strafford produced, besides Browning's play, the three so-called "Cavalier Tunes" which have been so often printed but so seldom sung. Browning was not the drinking-song kind of poet. The social and political life of England was recorded more memorably in his attack on Wordsworth. Browning, still giving his formal allegiance to Shelley and to Shelley's belief that poets were the "unacknowledged legislators of mankind," judged that the seventy-five-year-old Poet Laureate had turned his back on the great constituency; and "The Lost Leader" was his interestingly heartless reprimand.

V *Triumphs of Time*

The Browning destined to wear the title "optimist" had not yet appeared on the scene. Preparing *Dramatic Romances and*

Lyrics in 1845, the poet failed to send "Night and Morning" to Elizabeth Barrett as he did other poems. Quite possibly he reasoned that the situation of the first part and the conclusion of the second would have distressed his friend. "Night and Morning" (later printed as two poems, "Meeting at Night" and "Parting at Morning") presents a carnal assignation in its first half, and insists upon the partial and temporary nature of the affair in its second. The "two hearts beating each to each" will have to go in their two separate directions afterwards; neither heart needs to expect many such nights; the rising sun lights the speaker's way back to "a world of man."

Such triumphs of time are insisted upon in several other poems of the early pamphlets. In "Earth's Immortalities," for example, the two major objectives of human effort are held to have no future. Does one work for fame?

> ... as the prettiest graves will do in time,
> Our poet's wants the freshness of its prime; ...
> [And] the minute grey lichens, plate over plate,
> Have softened down the crisp-cut name and date.

Love, the other "immortality," is equally certain to dissolve. Hopes of March, April, and May ripen into "June's fever," a sickness terminating in "snows" which "fall round me." A plaintive second voice which Browning prints in italics keep calling out *"Love me for ever,"* but the main speaker can only answer, "The year's done with." In another poem of parting, "The Lost Mistress," Browning causes his speaker to suggest that love will "stay in my soul for ever." But the poet does so only to present the sad argument that was presented in "Cristina," for the love is similarly one-sided, and the other party knows it will end.

Some different attacks on the problem of time occur in the two earliest of Browning's famous observations on Renaissance painting. The shorter of the two is "Pictor Ignotis," which in translation becomes the catalogue-tag, "painter unknown." "Pictor Ignotis" is a painterly counterpart to Arnold's "Scholar-Gypsy." The uncompetitive, institutionally-oriented painter who narrates compares his own faithful but routine work to the inventive, colorful, naturalistic work of ego-oriented "new men" of the Renaissance, the hard men eager to compete for cash and fame. The money nexus and the "prate" of "vain tongues" would soil his artistic chastity:

> If at whiles
> My heart sinks, as monotonous I paint
> These endless cloisters and eternal aisles
> With the same series, Virgin, Babe, and Saint,
> With the same cold calm beautific regard,—
> At least no merchant traffics on my heart;
> The sanctuary's gloom at least shall ward
> Vain tongues from where my pictures stand apart.

The competitive and sensual bearing of the artistic mind of the Renaissance is developed in "The Bishop Orders his Tomb in St. Praxed's Church." John Ruskin, the dean of critics of Renaissance arts, immediately praised this poem as being the supreme summary of "the Renaissance spirit,—its worldliness, inconsistency, pride, hypocrisy, ignorance of itself, love of art, of luxury, and of good Latin." Elizabeth Barrett elected it the gem of the *Dramatic Romances*, and Browning himself called it his "pet."[3] Its single scene, the candlelit deathbed of the worldly bishop, soon became as well known as any scene in British poetry. Liar, thief, arsonist, fornicator, and simoniac, the bishop maintains to the end his jealousy, his greed, and his richly informed esthetics, focusing each upon art rather than upon religion. His own notion of Paradise is to "lie through the centuries" in the church he has filled with beautiful objects. At the end, dying, he loses the power to distinguish himself from the splendid recumbent statue he hopes his sons will build over him:

> For as I lie here, hours of the dead night
> Dying in state and by such slow degrees,
> I fold my arms as if they clasped a crook.
> And stretch my feet forth straight as stone can point,
> And let the bedclothes, like a mortcloth, drop
> Into great laps and folds of sculptor's-work.

His immortality will need to be in the art which surrounds him and to which he longs to attach himself. No other immortality can he imagine.

VI   *Christmas, Easter, and Silence*

While the *Dramatic Romances and Lyrics* were in progress, Browning developed his relationship with Elizabeth Barrett. On January 10, 1845, he addressed his first letter to her, saying among other things "I love your verses... and I love you too." The romance gradually developed from letters to visits to plans, and finally, on September 19, 1846, to an elopement in the general direction of Italy. Browning was thirty-three; his new wife was a semi–invalid of forty. Unquestionably, he was partly in flight from his mother and she from her father, and speculative psychology might insist that each had enrolled the other as a substitute for the person left behind. They were finally to settle in Florence, in a spacious flat in a house called "Casa Guidi." Since Elizabeth had money in her own name, as well as wealthy connections, Browning was regarded as a fortune-hunter by some persons. Their elopement was the talk of European literary circles for several months, and gradually broadened into a serious romantic equation for the literate middle classes of England and America. The wife was then a better-known poet than the husband and improved her competitive position as a poet during the years of their marriage. For a time, in 1850, she was touted as the likeliest choice to succeed Wordsworth as Poet Laureate. Tennyson won the laurels. Browning was hardly thought of, even by himself.

His ambitions were now uxorious. His devotion to his wife had become almost total; he praised her as the real poet of the household; he wrote little himself, and hardly published at all. The one significant thing he put forward during the whole decade of 1846-1855 was the volume containing *Christmas Eve* and *Easter Day*, and even that was better attuned to his wife's interests than to his own. The poem manifested in particular her often-repeated injunction that he stop being "dramatic" and speak boldly in his own voice—"to speak yourself out of the personality which God made, and which He turned into such power and sweetness of speech."[4] Elizabeth Barrett was, moreover, a passionate advocate of the evangelical and nonconforming Protestant version of Christianity which Browning's mother had advocated, and wished him to carry on that evangel. Browning's mood was triply haunted, late in 1849, by the death of his mother, the sickness and weakness of his wife, and the birth of his son Penini towards whom

he immediately felt jealous and rejecting. But by Christmas
of 1849, shaken out of his sloth, he was at work on his little
new volume, and it was published at Eastertide of 1850.

Christmas Eve and *Easter Day* are uttered in the "own
voice" of a wry, ironic, sometimes impatient young man whose
mission it becomes to assess evangelical Protestantism, Roman
Catholicism, and scholarly atheism. Although established as
the characteristic and traditional mode of British faith, the
eclectic "middle way" version called Anglican or Episcopal
was not even alluded to. Both poems are written in easy, shambling, comically rhymed couplets, ornamented with a great
deal of descriptive writing about "nature," most significantly
in the form of landscapes and skyscapes. Since *Christmas Eve*
has 1368 lines and *Easter Day* 1040, the book was a slim
one.

In *Christmas Eve*, Browning presents his speaker as entering
a tiny Protestant chapel in a bad slum. His only object is refuge
from a rainstorm in the street. He finds, sitting with him in
a tawdry little room, the wretched offscourings of urban
humanity—a fat harridan, a man with a large wen, a battered
city whore, a dirty adolescent far gone in consumption. Their
clergyman is ignorant, ungrammatical, and incapable of clear
thought. The visitor is offended and angered by the physical
squalor of the place, the "hot smell and human noises" of
the worshippers, and "the preaching man's stupidity" directed
towards "his audience's avidity." Rising in disgust, he goes
forth, and finds himself clutching the hem of the garment of
our lord Christ. By this handhold he is drawn to Rome, where
he witnesses with a mixture of awe and scorn the liturgical
magnificence of a high Christmas mass in St. Peter's. From
there he is drawn to the University of Göttingen, where a
professor with laryngitis is expounding the polite atheism then
called "Straussism" or "the higher criticism."

Tired from his attempt to evaluate the three religious systems, the speaker sits down and attempts an eclectic neutrality.
But sitting still, enjoying his "tolerance" and "mild indiffer-
entism," he discovers that the hem of Christ's vestment is
disappearing over the horizon. Suddenly in panic he leaps
to retrieve his grip on it. And behold, he wakes; it was all
a dream. The squalid worshippers in their miserable chapel
are eyeing him with insolent scorn; and the sermon, still igno-

rant, ugly, and paranoid, is still in progress. But it is this ratty congregation, the awakened Browning decides, which is performing the true religous service:

> Ask, else, these ruins of humanity,
> This flesh worn out to rags and tatters,
> This soul at struggle with insanity
> Who thus take comfort. . . .
> And let us hope
> That no worse blessing befall the Pope,
> Turned sick at last of today's buffoonery,
> Of posturings and petticoatings. . . .
> Nor may the Professor forego its peace
> At Gottingen presently, when in the dusk
> Of his life, if his cough, as I fear, should increase,
> Prophesied of by that horrible husk—
> When thicker and thicker the darkness fills
> The world through his misty spectacles
> And he gropes for something more substantial
> Than a fable, myth, or personification.

Though set up in honorific terms, the argument is the same as that which Marx was just then presenting pejoratively, and which, in fact, both Pope and Professor would have agreed to in their different ways. That Christianity arises in response to human desire has scarcely been doubted by anyone who has considered the problem. That it may arise from true, objective intervention by a true, objective divinity is the more knotty question which Browning did not take up.

Easter Day consists of roving dialogue on the proposition that it is "very hard . . . to be/A Christian." Browning's arguments are similar to those of St. Paul in Galatians and elsewhere, concerning salvation by faith. A few items of extrinsic interest occur. We learn, for example, that the lucubrations which have led to its conclusions have consumed "three years time," which would take their genesis back to the time of Browning's marriage to Elizabeth Barrett. Again, the speaker makes a charmingly uncandid disclaimer of experience in the wretched little chapel of which "our friend spoke . . . the other day." Childhood fears which the author may have had are reflected in a reminiscence of being

           little prone
For instance, when I lay alone
In childhood, to go calm to sleep
And leave a closet where might keep
His watch perdue some murderer
Waiting for twelve oclock to stir,
As good authentic legends tell.

Browning's way, he says, was not to cringe fearfully in bed.
He "would always burst/The door open, know my fate at first."
And at a couple of points when his arguments seem to drag,
he intrudes, using a remarkably unexpected metaphor, a personal vision or revelation which he had found convincing:

           So hapt
My chance. HE stood there. Like the smoke
Pillared o'er Sodom, when day broke,—
I saw Him. One magnific pall
Mantled in massive fold and fall
His head, and coiled in snaky swathes
About His feet.

But these are the lively spots in a not very inspiring poem.
In spite of swift and inventive versification, the vigor of *Christmas Eve* is absent from *Easter Day*. The presentation of abstract
argument in verse has been handled successfully by only a
handful of British writers—Dryden, Pope, and a few more;
and Browning, with his stronger dependence on persons and
events, does not qualify for leadership in that function.

CHAPTER 5

Men and Women: *The "Subjective"*

I *"Objective and Subjective"*

IN 1855, after ten years of marriage to an emotionally demanding woman, and after a concurrent ten years of relative silence as a poet, Browning returned to England from
Italy to see *Men and Women* through the press. The two green-
clad volumes of *Men and Women* contain some fifty poems
plus a dedicatory epilogue, the well-known "One Word More,
to E. B. B." As in the collective volumes of a decade earlier,
Browning offered a bewildering variety of forms, themes,
styles, and characters; and a dozen of these new poems represent the peak of his creative achievement. Distance and silence
had endangered his career as a British poet, and he hoped
that the new book would "set [his] poetical house in order."[1]
It did not, and as he contemplated the tepid reviews and slow
sales he realized that it would not. Returning to Italy, he
watched his wife's new book *Aurora Leigh* become a runaway
best seller. To the British reader, he was still the lesser of
the two poets.

Among the perceptive reviews of *Men and Women* was one
by the French critic Joseph Milsand who drew attention to
a certain persistent mashing together of the "sources of
inspiration" of Browning's work. After explaining the dichoto-
mous terms "subjective" and "objective," Milsand wondered
whether Browning had not reached the victory of synthesis,
"so as to be, not in turn, but simultaneously, lyric and dramatic,
subjective and objective."[2] To make such a judgment was to
tread on dangerous ground, for Browning had once more given
warning that the speakers in his poems did not speak for him.
The occasion was a prose essay intended to appear as a preface
to a volume of the letters of Shelley. In this essay, Browning
had given great emphasis to the dichotomy "objective" and
"subjective," which is to say persons who spoke of and through

63

their environments and persons who dealt chiefly in inward experience. As we have seen, Browning's own claim, after *Sordello*, was to be "objective" or, in his more usual term, "dramatic."

The poet's disavowal of opinions expressed in his poems was more strongly stated in "One Word More for E. B. B.," the dedicatory poem of *Men and Women*. As most people know, "One Word More" embodies the conceit of artistic media shifted in response to personal emotion. In honor of the women they loved, Raphael had dropped the brush to write a sequence of sonnets, and Dante had forgone poetry to "paint an angel." Browning refuses to go quite so far:

> I stand on my attainment.
> This of verse alone, one life allows me;
> Verse and nothing else have I to give you.

Still he offers his wife this poem, written in trochaic pentameter blank lines, as her own unique possession, for its metrics are "lines I write the first time and the last time." The trope is now finished; the compliment has been paid; but the poet will not stop. Readers must not think, he continues, that lyric subjectivism may be found anywhere else in the book:

> Love, you saw me gather men and women,
> Live or dead or fashioned by my fancy,
> Enter each and all, and use their service,
> Speak from every mouth,—the speech a poem.
> Hardly shall I tell my joys and sorrows,
> Hopes and fears, belief and disbelieving;
> I am mine and yours, the rest be all men's,
> Karshook, Cleon, Norbert, and the fifty.

It is only "this once," that is in "One Word More," that he will "speak ... in my true person." The passage concludes with the often-quoted statement, "Where the heart lies, let the mind lie also," and with a hasty veering off into a disquisition about the moon and "my moon of poets." In the end, we seem to be being asked to forget the question of who is "speaking" when Browning is writing in verse.

A critic may, however, elect to stay with the dichotomy so carefully postulated by the poet and his reviewer. In terms of this dichotomy, the poems of *Men and Women* divide into a group of subjective or "lyrical" poems virtually all of which bear upon love experiences, and a contrasting group of quite objective, or "dramatic" poems, based, for the most part, on general culture and reading. Though perhaps not so rich as their cousins in the objective group, the lyrical poems offer a quite full spectrum of emotional experience. The range from "One Word More" and "My Star" to "Misconceptions" and "Two in the Campagna" is wide indeed. But the whole range may nearly fall within the real emotional experiences of Browning in his marriage, his friendships, and his personal feelings and opinions.

II *Garlands of Girls*

Browning's studies of love run the whole gamut of types from simple metaphors built into songs to analyses of the most profound and complex sort. Good examples of the first category are "My Star" and "Misconceptions," two of the shortest poems in *Men and Women.* The former lyric, which is distinguished by its oddly asymmetrical form, cites a star which is visible to the poet alone, and which, unlike other stars, "dartles" the two colors blue and red. Friends who "would fain see too" this extraordinary star, get views of the larger, more imposing Saturn. But—"What is it to me if their star is a world?/Mine has opened its soul to me; therefore I love it." "Misconceptions," one of Browning's most singable lyrics, compares a hopeful branch and a hopeful lover upon which a merely sojourning bird and sojourning Queen rest for an ecstatic moment before passing on. Both poems stress the sacrificial nature of loves which are great and true, but defectively one-sided.

"The Last Ride Together" is a masterpiece of ten eleven-line stanzas which somehow manage to combine swift movement with intense reflection. In this poem also, the adored girl has said a final "no." But she has agreed to go on a final canter through green fields; and as the journey progresses, the speaker (or nonspeaker, this time) contemplates the various possibilities of the lives of men, and settles on the bitter truth that all these possibilities must end in failure:

Fail I alone in words and deeds?

> Why, all men strive and who succeeds? . . .
> Look at the end of work, contrast
> The petty Done with the Undone vast,
> This present of theirs with hopeful past!
> I hoped she would love me. Here we ride.

The ride is as temporary as the star's glister or the delight of the branch and lover. But, even in its brevity, it is triumphant: "I gave my youth—but we ride, in fine."

"A Pretty Woman" and "A Light Woman" are studies not so much of their title characters as of the man who talks about these characters. In real life, the "pretty" woman was an American expatriate whom the Brownings had found physically delightful but banal and flat in character. In the poem, Browning advocates the possibility that the woman's beauty is in itself a sufficient crown of her personality. For her, indeed, the depth and passion which would ornament another woman might be disfiguring. If not disfiguring, such additions might "perfect" the girl. Browning was, as indicated elsewhere, steadily developing the opinion that perfected things are dead, and that only the not-yet-finished phenomena of life or art give point or purpose to human effort. "Is the creature too imperfect, say?/Would you mend it/And so end it?" he asks of this incomplete human being. In the more familiar poem "A Light Woman," the speaker blames himself for meddling in a satisfactory though probably impermanent sexual relationship. His inexperienced "friend" has fallen in love with an experienced and venturesome woman, the veteran of some "ninety and nine" former conquests. To "save" the friend, our man makes love to the woman and wins her. But now his friend loathes him; the woman, when she discovers his motives, will loathe him; and, "so far at least as I understand," he can scarcely escape loathing himself. "'Tis an awkward thing," he concludes, "to play with souls."

The element of guilt does not occur on the surface of either "Mesmerism" or "Women and Roses." What does occur is the dark, trancelike compulsions of true reveries and dreams, where guilt may lie with other emotions far under the surface. "Mesmerism" may have a connection with the approving interest which Elizabeth Browning, though not Robert Browning, felt towards Spiritualism and the occult. Browning tells his rather long story in swift, often witty, short-lined stanzas, a daring measure considering that the subject is the drawing, by sheer mesmeric will power, of the soul and body of a woman out of the "leaden line" of her coffin and into the arms of her former lover. "Women and Roses" represents an actual or imagined reverie in which three collections of women successively enter and leave the consciousness of the poet. Sometimes these women are spoken of as "roses three"; elsewhere, they are masses of blossoms. Single or multiple, the three floral images stand for women of the past, women of Browning's own present, and women who will rule things in the future. "All to one cadence/They circle their rose on my rose-tree," he says repeatedly. No very exact image is presented, but the symbolism seems deliberately yonic-phallic. The general thesis, that of perpetual longing appetites and perpetual failure of a satisfactory fulfillment, is perfectly clear.

The idea for the celebrated poem "Evelyn Hope" sprang from the death of a real girl. Critics have increasingly tended to dismiss this poem as an exercise in the Victorian sentimentality about nubile virgins, or as a bargain-basement profession of Christian faith in a heaven where parted spirits may meet again. What it really expresses is Browning's insatiable appetite for emotional experience. In the dead Evelyn, he recognizes more than anything else his own missed opportunity to love her. His words to her, should they meet again in another sphere, will be words of simple greed:

> I have lived, I shall say, so much since then,
>   Given up myself so many times,
> Gained me the gains of various men
>   Ransacked the ages, spoiled the climes;
> Yet one thing, one, in my soul's full scope
>   Either I missed, or itself missed me—
> And I want and find you, Evelyn Hope.

And he will "take" her, too. He has coveted "the frank young smile/And the red young mouth and the hair's young gold"; and his pressing of a geranium leaf into her cupped dead hand plainly symbolizes a sexual connection. But the experience he laments having missed is much more than a sexual experience. Just as to the young sculptor in "Youth and Art," the opportunity for a vivid personal relationship has presented itself to him; and, through inaction, he has "missed it, lost it forever."

III   *Comparative Studies*

In another and more interesting line of argument, Browning made deliberate comparisons between double sets of potentials. In some poems following this line, for example, the poems "In Three Days" and "In a Year," the resulting disparities are not completely realized, perhaps because of the multiplicity of new elements placed in the second unit to generate the disparity. In others, and most notably in the masterpieces "Love among the Ruins" and "Two in the Campagna," the structures from which disparity appears are more clearly stated; and the analyses consequently are more telling.

The poem "In Three Days" offends exact people by using the word "day" to mean both daytime and the twenty-four-hour legal day. The poem expresses the wild impatience of a lover who is waiting for some deliriously important tryst, or perhaps for an elopement:

> I shall see her in three days
> And one night, now the nights are short,
> Then just two hours, and that is morn.

If elopement is indeed meant, the "morn" would stand for the beginning of a new and bright life, not just a new day. By that standard, the companion poem "In a Year" is all sunset. Now it is the woman who speaks, and she finds the man's embraces "bitter," his love "grown chill," and his previously passionate heart "a cold grey clod." The male-female difference in quality and endurance of love is given very explicitly. The woman has put into her lover's hand not only her life's assets ("Beauty, youth/Wealth and ease") but her whole ego and consciousness. In exchange, he has given her "his love"; but after a year of marriage, she discovers that his love was only temporary. "Love's so different with us men," she makes him say.

"One Way of Love" and "Another Way of Love" are linked as much by their titles and positioning as by their contents, which are more sketchily in contrast. In the first poem, the male speaker claims to have offered everything to his beloved—his possessions (called "roses" in the poem) and his skills (called "lute-playing"), and now asks for the verdict— "Heaven or hell?" When the unresponsive lady will not give him "Heaven," he responds with the calm magnanimity of an honest and solid man. In "Another Way of Love" Browning provides three main integers: a bantering woman, a listening man, and a metaphoric "June" which stands for a Love abstracted from both. The man, "with a man's true air," has led the woman to think that the perfections of June may be getting tiresome. The woman responds, with a humor opposite to the despair of the similarly situated woman of "In a Year," that the man should seek other forms of fun. A little change will be good for her too—"If June mends her bowers now, your hand left unsightly/By plucking their roses—my June will do rightly." She even suggests, though a bit cryptically, that a certain "One" more appreciative of June may turn up:

> ... for pastime
> If June be refulgent
> With flowers in completeness ...
> And choose one indulgent
> To redness and sweetness
> ... Why, June will consider.

The speaker's bantering threats leave no doubt about her capacity to survive neglect, and perhaps to avenge it.

A certain obscurity does haunt "Love in a Life" and "Life in a Love." Modern writers on Browning, who have tended to back away from these two poems, have sometimes tripped and fallen in the process. I find it impossible to improve upon Mrs. Orr's two short paragraphs:

> "Love in a Life" represents the lover as inhabiting the same house with his unseen love; and pursuing her in it ceaselessly from room to room, always catching the flutter of her retreating presence, always sure that the next moment he will overtake her.
>
> "Life in a Love" might be the utterance of the same person, when he has grasped the fact that the loved one is determined to elude him. She may baffle his pursuit, but he will never desist from it, though it absorb his whole life.

The difficulty in understanding the two poems as clearly as

Mrs. Orr did seems to have arisen from the general unwillingness of Browning critics and readers to admit the complexity
and occasional duplicity of the Brownings in their married-
lover roles. The poems offer a situation at odds with the
received view of the two poets as perfectly matched and perfectly in love. They belong to the class of poems which Browning would instantly declare to be "dramatic" in the sense of
speaking for some other person, not himself.

By far the most mated of the paired poems are two which
Browning himself did not juxtapose in *Men and Women*. Both
"Love among the Ruins" and "Two in the Campagna" are
set in a fair outdoors country dotted with ruins dating from
pre-Roman antiquity. The young speaker of "Love among the
Ruins" walks through "solitary pastures" which were "the
site once of a city great and gay,/ ... Of our country's very
capital." But the speaker's interest is actually "a girl with eager
eyes and yellow hair" whom he is to find in the "single little
turret" which is all that remains of a lofty structure upon which
the amphitheater, the city, and the empire have centered:

> Oh heart! Oh blood that freezes, blood that burns,
>   Earth's returns
> For whole centuries of folly, noise, and sin!
>   Shut them in
> With their triumphs and their glories and the rest.
>   Love is best!

Browning placed this poem at the very beginning of *Men and
Women* with the clear intention of establishing a high, youthful,
positive note at the beginning.

The companion poem, "Two in the Campagna," is placed
in the most desolate part of Volume Two, between "The Heretic's Tragedy" and "The Grammarian's Funeral." Like its
neighbors it speaks of death. "Rome and May," says the
speaker, have vanished. The speaker now wishes to discuss
"a thought" which "has tantalized me many times," and the
main structure of the poem arises from the pursuit of that
thought. The girl has wanted love to be "best" or "all." The
man's "thought" is that human perception cannot sustain the
ecstatic wholeness of which it is capable in hours of passion.
Love is not "under our control." Passion is a matter of "good
minutes." Fixed union is impossible—as the title sug-

gests—and love is simply not enough to fill a man's life. "The good minute goes." The abstracted passion, he concludes, may have been "infinite," but the yearning hearts are merely finite; and from this difference arises the agonies of our loves.

IV *Couples*

Contrary to Browning's admonition in "One Word More" and elsewhere, an interesting group of poems which refer to couples may be usefully read in the context of the lives of the Brownings. One or two maintain a general cheerfulness. In "Respectability," for example, the poet celebrates the unconventional delights available to persons who have "found out the world" and learned to ignore "the world's good word." The scene is Paris and the allusion is to an elopement such as that of the Brownings. Four other poems of *Men and Women* go more deeply into the lives of couples whose experiences reflect the known experiences of the two poets.

"A Woman's Last Word" and "A Lover's Quarrel" present us with marital differences. The "last word" of the speaker in the first poem is directed against any further words:

> Let's contend no more, Love,
> Strive nor weep—
> All be as before, Love,
> —Only sleep.

She promises complete submission, and will ("tomorrow/Not tonight") meet any demand of his for "flesh or spirit." This female strategy of victory through delayed surrender controls most other elements of the attractive little monologue. The man who is the speaker in "A Lover's Quarrel" is more humorous, and brings a wider field of speculation into his discourse. The situation he presents, however, seems much more serious. In early stanzas he reminisces about the good times he has shared with his lover. Every event was then sweet—the morning paper, a book about Argentina, experiments with the occult, and little joking masquerades. That was in winter "three months ago/When we lived blocked up with snow." Since then some deviltry has "Pierced to our ingle-glow,/And the friends were friend and foe!" The satanic shaft was oral again, "a bubble born of breath," only one "hasty

word." Now the weather is better, but the speaker faces an
empty spring and a barren summer. Curiously, his dreams
for reunion evoke a "bare-walled crypt" in the frigid air of
which the couple might be reunited. A close look may convince
many readers that the poem reflects a serious, long-lasting
disturbance in Casa Guidi.

In "Any Wife to Any Husband" a dying woman invokes
a set of premises which prove to her that her soon-
to-be-bereaved husband must never marry again. Browning
lets her speak in a strange archaic language, hyper-literary
but also close to prose:

> Oh, three parts through the worst of life's abyss,
> What plaudits from the next world after this
> Could'st thou repeat a stroke and gain the sky!

A delightful counterpoise to this weepy item exists in "By
the Fireside," another poem on wife-worship. "By the
Fireside" is structured around the sharing of a hearth-fire by
a silent couple years past their youth. The wife sits "Musing
by the firelight, that great brow/And the spirit-small hand
propping it/Yonder, my heart knows how." The man pretends
to read Greek, but he is, in fact, filling out the structure by
moving through two parallel reveries about a walking trip in
the Italian Alps. In the first reverie he describes the terrain
in terms of the triumphant union of the two lovers who have
walked across it. As Wordsworth might have done, he uses
his landscape not only as a background but as an active force
for the courtship:

> The forests had done it; there they stood—
>   We caught for a second the powers at play:
> They had mingled us so, for once and for good,
>   Their work was done—we might go or stay,
> They relapsed to their ancient mood.

It is interesting that the forests had done their work by the
mechanism of threat. Their sights and sounds, "the lights and
the shades," had "made up a spell/Till the trouble grew and
stirred." The woman, not the man, takes the lead in the emotional exchange which ends the trouble—something that had
happened even in Wimpole Street and which happened

repeatedly after the Brownings' elopement. But the poem as art transcends the poem as biography. With its leisurely fifty-three stanzas, its intense concern with environmental influences, its mature warmth and sobriety, and its extraordinarily graceful workmanship, "By the Fireside" is among Browning's finest poems.

V *Deviations of Object*

A final set of poems from *Men and Women* in which Browning speaks his own mind through his own speech falls outside of the themes of sexual love. This group includes "Memorabilia," "De Gustibus—," "Popularity," and "Transcendentalism," all of which vend his special likings and opinions, and "The Guardian Angel," one of his most intimately personal autobiographical pieces.

Not much needs to be said about "Memorabilia." The poem reflects back to Browning's hero-worship of Shelley, and shows through a simple parallel how one meeting with the "sun-treader" might stand as the most monumental event in a man's life. "De Gustibus—" (from the Latin maxim *De Gustibus non est disputandum,* or "There's no accounting for tastes")—is really two poems, each of which supposes that the regional preferences of a living man may be freely maintained by the man's ghost. Thus, the ghost of one, a "lover of trees," will haunt "(If loves remain)/An English lane,/By a cornfield side a-flutter with poppies." Browning's own ghost will seek his foster-nation Italy. In a few lovely lines he salutes the Italian weather and rough scenery, the Italian food, populace, and politics. The very name "Italy," he says, borrowing his metaphor from the militant Queen Mary, is engraved on his heart. "De Gustibus" is thus in the line of "Home Thoughts from Abroad" and "The Englishman in Italy"; but in its vividness and high spirits it surpasses both.

"Popularity" and "Transcendentalism" are versifications of critical maxims affecting poetry. In the first four stanzas of "Popularity" Browning expresses sympathy for a "true poet" whose work, unfortunately, nobody reads. In the next six stanzas he expounds upon the manufacture and distribution of the dyestuffs which, originating as mere sea-shells, were merchandised by Tyre throughout the ancient world. In the final three stanzas he brings poem-making and dye-making sharply together:

> Mere conch! not fit for warp or woof!
>   Till art comes,—comes to pound and squeeze
> And clarify,—refines to proof
>   The liquor filtered by degrees,
> While the world stands aloof.
>
> And there's the extract, flasked and fine,
>   And priced, and saleable at last!
> And Hobbs, Nobbs, Stokes, and Nokes combine
>   To paint the future from the past,
> Put blue into their line.
>
> Hobbs hints blue,—straight he turtle eats.
>   Nobbs prints blue,—claret crowns his cup.
> Nokes outdares Stokes in azure feats,—
>   Both gorge. Who fished the murex up?
> What porridge had John Keats.

The full name of the other tutelary poem is "Transcendentalism: a Poem in Twelve Books." An opus under this name, the project of a brother poet, has sought to versify "stark-naked thought" on the premise that "grown men want thought . . . /Thought's what they mean by verse, and seek in verse." Browning objects that honest poetry does not proceed from a poet's "thought" or "reason" but from his imagination and his desire to create. His not very apposite instance of the arid and tiresome mere thinker is the mystic Jacob Boehme. His worker on the other side is John of Halberstadt, a "stout mage" who "made things Boehme only thought about." "Song's our art," he concludes, and song is not thinking but creation.

These poems, in spite of their seeming simplicity, tell us a great deal about Browning's views of his art. In "The Guardian Angel: a Picture at Fano," he presents a most unusual view of himself. Scattered through the poem are allusions to the most personal kind of data: his journeys, his wife, his old friend Alfred Domett, even the drowning of Joseph Arnould "where rolls the Wairoa." The picture which motivated this self-review is by Guercino, and depicts an enormous, white-winged angel who is giving affection and instruction to an infant held in her lap. Browning imagines himself as replacing the infant and lying safe against the warm bosom of the angel:

If this was ever granted, I would rest
     My head beneath thine, while thy healing hands
Close-covered both my eyes beside thy breast,
     Pressing the brain, which too much thought expands,
Back to its proper size again, and smoothing
Distortion down till every nerve had soothing,
     And all lay quiet, happy and supprest.

Such a poem is easily used against a poet. Thus Betty Miller in her biography draws from it to "show" that Browning's personality was morbidly infantile and passive-dependent.[3] In the context of his entire surging product, its data can hardly lead to such an interpretation. But it does show Browning in an uncharacteristic state of weariness, anxiety, and over-strain; and it remains among the most intimately personal of all his poems.

CHAPTER 6

Men and Women:
The Almost Objective

I *Limits of the Objective*

FILLED as the poems are with carefully distinguished other speakers and with situations outside the experience of Browning, the remaining half of the poems of *Men and Women* may with some fairness be called "objective." Since before adopting the term "objective" Browning had tended to use "dramatic" with the same meaning, it is interesting that, of all the poems of *Men and Women*, he came closest to the ideal of objectivity in the longish production "In a Balcony," which takes the form of a regular play.

"In a Balcony" has only three characters: the lovers Norbert and Constance, and an otherwise nameless Queen, a lady of fifty who has married badly, selflessly given herself to politics, and never known love. As the play begins, we find that the Queen has come to love her well-deserving Prime Minister, Norbert. But Norbert loves the Queen's niece Constance, who also loves him. There have been trysts, assignations, and secret nocturnes; but, as the play opens, Norbert is found demanding an open courtship and marriage. Constance is convinced that the Queen will be jealous unless the declaration is made in a certain way—that is, Norbert is to tell the Queen that he loves her royal self and that he wants to marry Constance only because of her closeness and dearness to the throne. Unknown to the lovers, the Queen has meant to marry them to each other; but now, seriously misconstruing the misconstruction presented by Norbert, she passionately accepts Norbert for herself. Nothing must stand in their way:

> [for] I
> Will drive those difficulties far and fast
> As yonder mists curdling before the moon.
> I'll use my light too, gloriously retrieve

> My youth from its enforced calamity,
> Dissolve that hateful marriage, and be his. . . .
> Why, how I baffle obstacles, spurn fate!
> How strong I am! (543-48, 566-7)

The explanation, when it comes, causes the proud Queen to sentence Norbert and Constance to death.

The cast, scene, and situation of "In a Balcony" are the sheerest of romantic froth. Browning himself did not trust the piece. In later editions he removed it from its place among the masterpieces of *Men and Women* and called it, in delicate disclaimer, "In a Balcony—a Scene." But the point is that this dramatic poem was truly "dramatic" or "objective" in the sense that its values came from a system for which Browning would not be spokesman. None of the poems which remain to be mentioned truly embody such a distinction. During his decade of near-silence, Browning had become a man of strong opinions—and of zeal to make his opinions prevail. We are not asked to blame either Andrea or Andrea's adulterous Lucrezia, and stupidity rather than cruelty is given emphasis in "Holy Cross Day" and "A Heretic's Tragedy." But points are given, and points are taken away; and except for a few comic pieces like "Up in the Villa, Down in the City," we are always asked to take a side.

II   *Testaments on the Arts*

The decade that followed "Pictor Ignotis" and "The Bishop Orders His Tomb" had deepened Browning's scholarship in the fine arts without blunting his enthusiasm for them. Visiting him in Paris in 1855, when *Men and Women* had just been published, the artist-poet Dante Gabriel Rossetti "found his knowledge of early Italian art beyond that of anyone I ever met,—*encyclopedically* beyond that of Ruskin himself."[1] Among the recently published poems, Rossetti had been most impressed by "Old Pictures in Florence," in which the encyclopedic learning of Browning is most fully deployed. It has been argued, indeed, that he had perfected a whole esthetic philosophy.

Rossetti was able to call "Old Pictures in Florence" a "jolly thing," but Caryle and other friends deplored it as containing so much learning and liberty that it turned away the common

reader. The speaker, a tough-talking, neo-Byronic type of critic,
looks out over Florence, has his attention caught by the Cam-
panile designed but not finished by the old major-minor artist
Giotto, and moves into a set of statements about his now-
familiar "doctrine of the imperfect" by alleging conceptual
differences which make such admittedly imperfect works
superior to the "perfection" of Greek art; about the necessity
of the knowledge of imperfection (Christianly oriented) to continual improvement in the arts; and (rather dragging it in)
about the coming of a great political epoch when the arts will
all revive and when Giotto's tower will be finished in the
free air of a liberated Italian Republic.

This orderly structure is nearly lost, however, under an ag-
gregate of biographical, critical, and historical detail of the
minutest kinds. The enormous weight of the poem is offset
by Browning's hail-fellow manner and by his most grotesquely
shambling versification:

> We'll shoot this time better game and bag 'em hot—
>   No display of the stone of Dante,
> But a kind of a Witan-agemot
>   ("Casa Guidi," *quod videas ante*)
> To ponder Freedom returned to Florence,
>   How Art may return that departed with her.
> Go, hated house, go each trace of the Loraine's!
>   And bring us the days of Orgagna hither.

A memorable feature of the poem is the cluster of tattered,
beaten, small ghosts whom Browning invokes near the beginning and recalls near the end. These are the spirits of ancient
minor masters who have been shoved aside by the great
geniuses of the High Renaissance. Smashed and jostled by
the force and learning of Browning, many readers tend to iden-
tify with these inferior artists.

"Fra Lippo Lippi" and "Andrea del Sarto" are pitched much
lower. Both are written in conversational first-person blank
verse but in different styles as demanded by the difference
between the two characters. Both are studies of degeneration
and failure. Brother Lippi, a drunken monk caught by a police
squad in a bordello alley, tells with tendentious jocularity how,
as a hungry child, he was taken into a monastery and under
threat of starvation forced to manufacture paintings wholly

at odds with his own esthetic philosophy. Lippo's own taste is for "real life": that is, worldliness in his career and naturalism in his painting. But, at the critical moment of his apprenticeship, his Prior has laid the law down oppositely:

> Your business is to not to catch men with show,
> With homage to the perishable clay,
> But lift them over it, ignore it all;
> Make them forget there's such a thing as flesh.
> Your business is to paint the souls of men—
> Man's soul, and it's a fire, smoke—no it's not—
> It's vapour done up like a new-born babe—
> (In that shape when you die it leaves your mouth)
> It's—well, what matters talking, it's the soul!
> Give us no more of body than shows soul.

Lippo's response to the Prior was to paint as vaguely as seemed desired; and, still doing so at the time of the monologue, he blames his spells of drinking and wenching upon the frustrations caused by his being made to follow irrational values. "I do these wild things in sheer despite," he says; "And play the fooleries you catch me at/In pure rage." Lippo's errors provide one of Browning's most lively people and most loved poems.

In sharpest contrast to the drunken rodomontade of Lippo's self-analysis is the beaten masochism of Andrea del Sarto's. The bad habit of del Sarto was not carousing but domestic fidelity. This "perfect painter" has ridden his exquisite mastery of technique to the high place of Court Painter to the King of France; but, because of his wife Lucrezia's whim, he has dropped out of the high competition, left France, and let his work decline to dead though perfect technique. He partly blames her and partly himself, but has grown so weary and thwarted as to have no strong convictions about it. He has been completely unmanned, in short, both as an artist and as a husband. In the end, when his wife leaves to cuckold him with a "cousin," he dreams of "heaven, perhaps, new chances":

> One more chance;
> Four great walls in the New Jerusalem
> Meted on each side by the angel's reed,

> For Leonard, Rafael, Angelo, and me
> To cover.

But the three titans would still "overcome," he sadly adds, since their aspirations remain greedy while he has settled for the mere cheap Lucrezia.

Two of the poems in *Men and Women* present discoveries about humanity through discussions of music. "Master Hugues of Saxe-Gotha" is written in the comic-grotesque manner Browning had used in "Old Pictures in Florence" and earlier in such poems as "The Pied Piper." Its speaker is a church organist who isolates himself in the organ-loft with the score of a fugue by an invented composer, Master Hugues. Fugues develop by the accumulation of parts or "voices" so as to produce a sort of musical debate. Browning's organist plays Hugues's parts as music but speaks of them as men—men in a debate which ultimately seems meaningless. As with del Sarto's two hundred paintings, all their value seems to lie in the fine technique. A sinister meaning develops from the emptiness of the composition with its "moral of life" reduced to a web of "impotent strife." The organist descends from the loft angry and frustrated by this merely mathematical kind of music.

There was a real Galuppi, and the speaker in the masterly poem "A Tocatta of Galuppi's" finds him wrong in approximately the same way as the unreal Hugues was wrong. Musical composition for Galuppi and other eighteenth-century Venetians had become, as Browning urges, a lifeless arithmetical exhibition, and its only valid message is that living things must die. The speaker, though "never out of England," is introduced to the cynical and pleasure-seeking works of eighteenth-century Venice by Galuppi's simple toccatta—to music, dancing, lovely women, lies, adulteries, and death. The final stanza is unsurpassed as a lyrical unit:

> Dust and ashes! So you creak it, and I want the heart to scold.
> Dear dead women, with such hair too—what's become of
> all the gold
> Used to hang and brush their bosoms? I feel chilly and grown old.

In "How it Strikes a Contemporary," Browning returns to

his own art of poetry. The speaker, a resident of Valladolid, describes a fellow-citizen whose only function seems to be observation of passing events:

> He stood and watched the cobbler at his trade,
> The man that slices lemons into drink,
> The coffee-roaster's brazier, and the boys
> That volunteer to help him turn the winch.
> He glanced o'er books on stalls with half an eye,
> The fly-leaf ballads on the vendor's string,
> And broad-edge, bold-print posters ·by the wall.
> He took such cognisance of men and things,
> If any beat a horse, you felt he saw;
> If any cursed a woman, he took note;
> Yet stared at nobody,—they stared at him.

A rich legendry had grown up around this man. Though poor and threadbare, he was thought to live a secret life of worth and power. It was said that he ate his meals "in a room/Blazing with lights, four Titians on the walls,/And twenty naked girls to change his plate." His function, as his fellow-citizens see it, must be that of a powerful spy or "recording chief-inquisitor."

> We merely kept a Governor for form;
> While this man walked about, and took account
> Of all thought, said, and acted, then went home
> And wrote it fully to our Lord the King,
> Who has an itch to know things.

His power, exerted through his supposed influence with the "King," must be immense: he must be "The town's true master, if the town but knew." At his death, the speaker imagines, the poet, or grand inquisitor, may put aside his shabby-genteel outfit and emerge in the glories of a "commander-in-chief" who concludes "a whole campaign of the world's life and death/Doing the King's work."

It would be hard to underestimate the significance of this rather short poem to Browning's thought about all arts and especially about poetry. The background facts date all the way back to Browning's adolescent reading. The combination of awe and doubt expressed by the speaker about the function of this strange man, the "one poet" known to him, is an extension of Browning's lifelong questioning and self-questioning on the subject. Was Shelley right in calling poets "the unacknowledged legislators of mankind?" The more tangible view Browning expressed in the abortive Shelley book and elsewhere was that poets were principally watchers and reporters: their function was that of "beholding with an understanding keenness the universe, nature, and man, in their actual state of perfection and imperfection." The Valladolid poet's supposed connection with "our Lord the King" is echoed by a sentence of Browning's in a letter to Ruskin: "A poet's affair is with God, to whom he is accountable, and of whom is his reward."[2] The isolation and suspicion with which poets are all too familiar would result naturally from any such command system.

III   *The Ethics of Resistance*

A half-dozen poems in *Men and Women* and a good many more in Browning's other books versify the ethical concept of simple but adamant resistance—a concept that has never been better explained than by Shelley in the closing stanzas of *Prometheus Unbound.* Shelley had postulated an individual forced to endure isolation, wrong, injury, and pain, who nevertheless found glory through mere unwillingness to acquiesce. The resolution of Prometheus "neither to change, nor falter, nor repent" was the governing factor in his gaining "Life, Joy, Empire, and Victory." A man may express his adamancy of character in any cause—good or bad, sensible or silly; for it is the adamancy itself and not the cause that is important. Simple resistance is an ethics on its own.

Browning's simplest statements about the ethics of resistance were made in "Instans Tyrannus" and "The Grammarian's Funeral." "Instans Tyrannus" may cheat a little, since in its surprise ending we learn that the supposedly isolated object of tyranny has after all had a friend ("God"). The poem is a monologue uttered by a great king or emperor who nurses an obsessive hatred toward one of his most abject subjects. Beaten, humiliated, tempted, "inveigled," and pointlessly imprisoned, the helpless victim groans and grovels but is not broken. The monarch is gradually driven frantic by "the thought of his face,/The droop, the low cares of the mouth,/The trouble uncouth/Twixt the brows." The reader never does know what the victim is supposed to do or not do, for the point is that the ugly wretch refuses.

Browning's well-known and often-interpreted poem "The Grammarian's Funeral" presents a far richer embroidering of the theme. The students who proudly bear their professor's corpse to a summit "where meteors shoot, clouds form/Lightnings are loosened" have cherished him for his pertinacious refusal to permit any activity, even rest, which would interfere with his studies. Once having chosen his discipline (Classical philology) and named "knowledge" as his objective, he had committed himself to a lifetime of hard work. Certain voices have tried to corrupt him: he is enjoined to "live," to "enjoy," or to change his objectives. He refuses. The approach of death has terrors, perhaps, but no professional impact:

> So, with the throttling hands of Death at strife,
>   Ground he at grammar;
> Still, through the rattle, parts of speech were rife.

Some critics have said that Browning may have been trying to express through irony a view opposite to that of the proud students. Such arguments are based on the supposed weakness of philology as the key to a man's existence. But "A Grammarian's Funeral" does not evaluate the various callings which men may follow; it evaluates a stubborn, singleminded human being, and finds him a hero.

Two other adjurations about constancy, and never mind the cause, exist in "The Statue and the Bust" and "Childe Roland to the Dark Tower Came." "The Statue and the Bust" caused a stir in its time because of its urging that the morality of consistent and determined action might override such rival moralities as wedded fidelity and political responsibility. Browning's illustrative story is simple, though undoubtedly too long. A reigning nobleman of Florence has fallen in love with a noblewoman newly a bride. They have decided upon adultery and elopement, retained the decision for year after inactive year, and finally let it freeze into a bust and statue which emptily stare at each other across the city square. Browning's view (that of a man who did elope) is that, upon making their decision, they should have acted at once. In any test of character, he argues, what really counts is one's decisive

behavior rather than the contents of one's decision. "As well
the counter as coin," he says—"If you choose to play." Having
chosen to play, these two Florentine lovers had already failed
in social morality. The only remaining test was a test of integrity, which they also failed.

The hero and speaker of "Childe Roland," a poem of much
greater depth and profundity, shambles into our view after
a whole series of torments and defeats. We follow Roland over
a weary, desolate landscape; and we hear him summarize the
matching desolation of his spirit. He is on some kind of quest,
but has lost all hope for its success. His dearest friends, whom
he names for us, have gone whirling off into disgrace and
death; and he expects no better for himself. His progress over
the horrible terrain becomes mere automatism and drift. Suddenly, within a ring of barren hills, he finds himself confronting
"the round squat turret" that has been his lifelong objective.
Something within the tower needs to be killed. But now, suddenly again, the heretofore silent desert is full of spirits and
spirit voices:

> Names in my ears,
> Of all the lost adventurers my peers,—
> How such a one was strong, and such was bold,
> And such was fortunate, yet each of old
> Lost! Lost! One moment knelled the woe of years.
> There they stood, ranged along the hillsides—met
> To see the last of me, a living frame
> For one more picture!

He still has the option of turning back, but the value of personal
integrity transcends that of survival; and we leave him blowing
a stubborn horn-blast in defiance of the turret-housed Unknown which will now destroy him.

Not only in the stage-clothes of the ancient and exotic did
Browning present the merit of steering straight forward. He
could also present it, perhaps with less sympathy, in the
sophisticated drama of contemporary top-level Roman Catholicism. "Bishop Bloughram's Apology," the longest monologue of the set, features a wealthy and powerful bishop
whose mission, as he sees it, is to establish the narrow ground
between cynical worldliness and heaven-looking piety.
Browning's model for the Bishop was Cardinal Wiseman, the

leading Roman Catholic clergyman in Britain at midcentury. Wiseman was later to be butchered by Lytton Strachey in *Eminent Victorians* for what Strachey took to be hypocrisy and intellectual sloth. Browning's exploration is more subtle and generous. He presents, almost as a prophetic anticipation of Strachey, a brash thirty-year-old journalist called Gigadibs who quite openly despises what he considers to be hypocrisy in the Bishop. Bloughram regales the lightweight writer with the finest food and wine, served in the Byzantine luxury of the episcopal palace, and utilizes the occasion to bewilder his intellect and pour contempt on his character. He laughs at the cheap simplicism of Gigadibs's idealistic pronouncements:

> You weigh and find, whatever more or less
> I boast of my ideal realized
> Is nothing in the balance when opposed
> To your ideal, your grand simple life,
> Of which you will not realize one jot.
> I am much, you are nothing; you would be all,
> I would be merely much. (79-85)

Admitting prior doubts of all sorts, he asserts that doubt has not been a satisfactory response to the difficulties of the human lot:

> The grand Perhaps! We look on helplessly.
> There the old misgivings, crooked questions are—
> This good God,—what he could do, if he would,
> Would, if he could—then must have done long since:
> If so, whom, where, and how? Some way must be,—
> Once feel about, and soon or late you hit
> Some sense, in which it might be after all.
> Why not? "The Way, the Truth, The Life?" (190-97)

The bishop finds such flimsy "reasonings" vulgar and silly. "You disbelieve!" he says to Gigadibs in open mockery: "Who wonders and who cares?"

A good half of the poem is composed of arguments to the effect that an intelligent belief must arise from intelligent choice and that a failure in unwilled belief by no means constitutes disbelief.

"What think ye of Christ," friend? When all's done and said
Like you this Christianity or not?
It may be false, but will you wish it true?
Has it your vote to be so if it can? . . .
If you desire faith—then you've faith enough. . . .
Pure faith indeed—you know not what you ask! (636-41, 647)

He concludes with another arraignment of the puritan Gigadibs, calling him a nobody, a bad writer, and a philosophic illiterate. In an interesting double conclusion, Browning first shows the Bishop systematically reviewing his own discourse. He has believed, he himself reports, about half of what he has said. The rest, he says, was "for argumentatory purposes" or else was "arbitrary accidental thoughts/Amusing because new." In other words, he may only have half believed in his own half-beliefs. In the second conclusion we find that Gigadibs has been so badly battered that he must emigrate to Australia and take up ranching. The fear and the sentimentality which have increasingly tinctured our appreciation of religious gambits have sadly limited the popularity of "Bishop Bloughram's Apology." It was possible for the real Cardinal Wiseman himself to call the poem "in its way triumphant,"[3] and it definitely is.

IV   Testaments of True Religon

Writing a bare generation ago, DeVane referred to "Saul" as "possibly more esteemed" than any other of Browning's poems. "Saul" and its religious cousins "Cleon" and "An Epistle of Karshish" attracted attention in their own time as "defenses" of religious faith against such attacks as those of Ernest Renan, David Friedrich Strauss, and the new breed of scientific humanists. The three poems maintained their position with ease in the period of Browning's own deification by English teachers and women's clubs; but, by a familiar backlash mechanism, they became, even while DeVane was writing, a sort of triple albatross rotting against the breast of his reputation. Currently, they are avoided with embarrassment.

Like their popular triumph, their falling out of popular favor is due to their message rather than their workmanship. In particular, "Saul" was the product of years of artistic thought and hard work. Its literary sources are the original story reported in I Samuel 16: 14–23, the eighteenth-century hymnist Christopher Smart's "Song to David," and Sir Thomas Wyatt's "Seven Penitential Psalms," a work dating from Tudor times. Browning's version was written in two thrusts, the first before 1845, when the results were shown to an admiring Elizabeth Barrett, and the second in early 1853, when Browning was revising some old productions for inclusion in *Men and Women.*

The first part presents, with bright imagery, the regular Old Testament biblical story of young David's being called to heal the insanity of King Saul through music. The second part, written much later (and beginning at Section 10), breaks into a sequence of theological paradoxes culminating in an intellectually generated burst of pure faith. At the core are the realization by David that, through love, he is capable of giving his life for Saul, and his consequent belief that a God, who would have greater powers and a greater responsibility, would through love do much more than he and for a greater number of persons. Such reasoning leads to post-prior predictions of the Christ ("See the Christ stand!") which need not convince persons not priorly convinced. But, even with the theology knocked away, the poem remains a singular invention. The figure of old man Saul, "drear and stark, blind and dumb," braced in shadows against the pole in the center of his tent, is especially memorable.

"Saul" is a very oral piece—a monologue spoken in reminiscence by David. "Cleon" and "An Epistle of Karshish" are in the form of letters. In the former, a Hellenistic intellectual writes to his monarch about life, creative activity, and death. Cleon's discourse is gradual and elegant, as befits a man who has achieved the perfection of Greek art and culture. Approaching his main point by several avenues, and finally laying it down as straight fact, the marvelously cultivated Cleon announces that the most significant fact of his cultural development is the awful knowledge that he must soon abandon it all:

> I, I, the feeling, thinking, acting man
> The man who loved his life so over much
> Shall sleep in his urn. It is so horrible.

Cleon's only hope would be the "something beyond" of advanced religion; but, if anything exists beyond, "Zeus has not yet revealed it; and alas!/He must have done so—were it possible." Ironically, Cleon must conclude his epistle with a business note about the difficulty of forwarding mail to "one called Paulus," a mumble-headed Jewish preacher "whose doctrine can be held by no sane man." Paul has the cure; Cleon is blind to it.

In the other great religious Epistle, the traveling scientist Karshish, writing to his revered professor in Arabia, reports his discoveries of strange flora and fauna in Palestine. One of the noteworthy specimens is a man, "one Lazarus, a Jew,/Sanguine, proportioned, fifty years of age." Lazarus's great distinction, besides salubrity, is his unique earlier experience of death and resurrection. Karshish attempts to subsume this experience under the term "case." Lazarus's "case" has manifested "mania, subinduced/By epilepsy, at the turning point/Of trance." The whole miracle of the resurrection is thus reduced to a compulsive delusion which Lazarus "hath gotten now so thoroughly by heart" that it returns continually as a fixed idea:

> And oft the man's soul springs into his face
> As if he saw again and heard again
> His sage that bade him "Rise" and he did rise.

Karshish's faith remains in physical science, but he cannot control his own compulsion to recur again and again to the experience of Lazarus and to the implications of it if it should prove to have been true. Thus science, speaking through Karshish, has reached the same halfway position as the humanities that spoke through Cleon.

Two poems in Browning's more grotesque vein handle Christianity through its behavioral opposites. In "The Heretic's Tragedy: a Middle-age Interlude," Browning creates a mock-antique colloquy about the execution by burning at the stake of John, Grand Master of the Knights Templars. "Interlude" implies a dramatic piece. Many voices join in chanting and response; and the intense vitality of sound, metaphor, and image culminate in a quite agonizing series of allusions to roses, beginning with the heavenly Rose of Sharon and

ending with the sickening image of John's body transmuted
to a rose:

> Ha, ha, John plucks now at his rose
>   To rid himself of a sorrow at heart!
> Lo,—petal on petal, fierce rays unclose;
>   Anther on anther, sharp spikes outstart;
> And with blood for dew, the bosom boils;
>   And a gust of sulphur is all its smell;
> And lo, he is horribly in the toils
>   Of a coal-black giant flower of Hell!

The chorus observes (against the poet's belief), "What maketh
Heaven, that maketh Hell."

Of equal energy, and with comedy and ethical judgments
superadded, is the poem called "Holy-Cross Day." On the
feast of that name, as Browning tells us in his notes, "the
Jews were forced to attend an annual Christian sermon in
Rome." The first spokesman in this poem is a "Bishop's
Secretary" whose bigotry yields a mocking prose version of
the event. The sixteen stanzas of the poem proper represent
"what the Jews really said." In the beginning, the crowding,
the jostling, and the ill temper of the forced worshippers is
given:

> Fee, faw, fum! bubble and squeak!
> Blessedest Thursday's the fat of the week!
> Rumble and tumble, sleek and rough,
> Stinking and savoury, smug and gruff,
> Take the church-road, for the bell's due chime
> Gives us the summons—'tis sermon-time.

This grumpy response moves into a recollected sermon of
"Rabbi ben Ezra, the night he died." Ben Ezra's words seem
to have been fierce and ugly. Christ himself is invoked as
judge of "The work of these dogs and swine,/Whose life laughs
through and spits at their creed,/Who maintain thee in word,
and defy thee in deed." Ben Ezra proceeds to still rougher
aspersions of Christian conduct, and is even more militant
than the Jews actually present. This Sermon of Death stands
in violent contrast to the agreeable philosophizing of the later
poem "Rabbi Ben Ezra."

V *Incidental Notes*

While not all of the moral tales of *Men and Women* are
as profound as "Childe Roland" or as lively as "Holy-Cross
Day," a sharp energy of theme and line enhances most of
them. Even in versifying a little anecdote about "date" and
"dabiture" ("give" and "take"), Browning could begin like
a tornado:

> Grand rough old Martin Luther
> Bloomed fables—flowers on furze,
> The better the uncouther.

The slight "fable" of Luther had been published earlier,
together with a poem of Elizabeth Barrett's, in a pamphlet
sold in support of working-class schools of London. The vigor
and ease are what make the poem.

New for *Men and Women* was an interlocking set of poems
celebrating a fatal duel. In "Before," a second, or observer,
describes the two duelists. One of them, he feels sure, is a
"culprit" whose movements are followed by a curious spotted
animal (called by some a "leopard of conscience" and by others
a mere stylish Dalmatian) which parallels its master with a
"leer and lie in every eye/On its obsequious hide." The other
duelist is a "martyred man." The speaker's word is that there
must be no bargaining or turning back, no forgiveness:

> All or nothing, stake it! trust to God or no?
> Thus far and no farther? Farther? Be it so.
> Now enough of your chicane and prudent pauses,
> Sage provisos, sub-intents, and saving-clauses.

His greed for instant and lethal action suggests the activistic
ethics of "The Statue and the Bust," but in this case there
is more to be said. The other poem of the set, "After" refers
to the hour following the duel, and the "true" duelist now
looks down on the body of the "culprit." He is not happy.
It has not struck him before that a dead man cannot be conscious of "his wrong nor my own vengeance." The lack of
comprehension in the corpse, as it turns out, has destroyed
the victory of the victor.

The two poems called "A Serenade at the Villa" and "Up

in the Villa, Down in the City" may be said to have flowered from the warm soil of Italy. The speaker or singer of "A Serenade" has spent the whole of an uncomfortable night singing love songs in the courtyard of his beloved. Now, at dawn, he tries to assess the effect. Has the lady learned from the music that there is one person whom, come day or night, heat or rain, she can always depend upon? Does she say—

> "One friend on the path shall be
>   To secure my steps from wrong;
> One to count night day for me,
>   Patient through the watches long,
> Serving most with none to see"?

His more devastating later thought is that his music has bored and annoyed her all night long. Does she call him a "plague" and ask only to "die in peace"? Probably. The villa itself shows hostility; it stands dark and forbidding, with "windows fast and obdurate," and an iron gate which "Ground its teeth to let me pass." "Up in a Villa, Down in the City" is the comic lament of "an Italian Person of Quality" against the poverty that keeps him in the former place. The charm of the poem comes from the convincingly naturalistic but lightly presented rural and civic data with which the "Person of Quality" compares the two environments.

The two poems "Protus" and "The Patriot" feature erosions of situations in the context of passing time. In "The Patriot" only a year needs to elapse. The speaker, an Italian revolutionary, is found entering Brescia in a victorious welter of scarlet:

> It was roses, roses all the way,
>   With myrtles mixed in my path like mad;
> The church spires flamed, such flags they had.

He behaves well in the new ruling group: "Nothing man could do have I left undone." But a political change in the ensuing year sweeps away all the roses:

> I go in the rain; and, more than needs,
>   A rope cuts both of my wrists behind;
> And I think, by the feel, my forehead bleeds,
>   For they fling, whoever has a mind
> Stones at me for my year's misdeeds.

The title character of "Protus" has been one of the "half-emperors and quarter-emperors" of the later Roman Empire. All that is left as evidence of Protus's brief rule is the sculptured bust of a baby and some bits of manuscript and scholarly gossip. The speaker sums up the known career of Protus, who reigned for a few months only, and tries to reconstruct the remainder of his life from shreds of academic garbage. Having been deposed, but perhaps left alive, Protus may have been a page or a schoolmaster "in some blind northern court," he may have written a treatise called "On Worming Dogs," or he may have become "a monk in Thrace" and died there full of years. The bust of his barbarian deposer, one "John of Pannonia, groundedly believed/A blacksmith's son" is displayed next to his. Ultimately, the contrast becomes visual. There is the imperial child, perfected, full of beauty and grace, "a baby face, with violets there/Violets instead of laurel in his hair." And here, right next, is the voracious aspirer whom Browning prefers:

> ... John the Smith's rough-hammered head. Great eye,
> Gross jaw and griped lips do what granite can
> To give you the crown-grasper. What a man!

CHAPTER 7

Wreck, Rebuild, and

Dramatis Personae

I *Wreck and Rebuild*

AFTER the publication and lukewarm reception of *Men and Women*, Browning returned via Paris to Florence, and commenced what was to register as the most barren period of his life. He did some editing of work by Mrs. Browning, and he reedited some of his own older work. For a while, he attempted a rewrite of *Sordello*, but the plan fell through. The little poem "May and Death" was printed in *The Keepsake*, a women's annual of a type then popular. But Browning's career energy still hung in suspense. His life with Mrs. Browning offered diminishing rewards. She was declining rapidly in health; the boy Penini was "hers" rather than the father's; the couple found itself increasingly at odds on such questions as Continental politics and the return of spirits from the land of the dead. During 1860, in a Florence marketplace, he picked up the old yellow-vellum-bound volume in which was recorded the brief marital adventure of Pompilia and Guido; and, as we shall see in the next chapter, he became emotionally and intellectually immersed in their agonies. But his own life became a hopeless round of journeys up and down Italy, of soothing and nursing his wife, and of the thrusts at music, painting, and sculpture with which he numbed his creative drive.

Finally, on June 29, 1861, Elizabeth Barrett died. Browning's epistolary professions of desolation do not escape over-emoting and over-writing. By contrast his practical behavior was quick and intelligent. The dead wife's money was quickly transferred to the live husband. Penini was shorn of his girlish locks and put into male attire; and his father dedicated himself, in letters, to making him "a manly English child."[1] Casa Guidi was stripped down to the plaster, and its total contents were boxed and shipped off to England. And in October, after a long rest with his father and sister on the coast of France, the poet established his residence at 19 Warwick Crescent in London.

Number 19 was a tall, narrow town house, distinctly middle-class, well situated a few doors from a squarish artificial pond where two canals crossed through each other. This home was to be Browning's for the next twenty-nine years. Still emotional and stagey in his bereavement, Browning filled the rooms with association pieces from Casa Guidi and elsewhere. One room was furnished "just as she had done it." Following the memorial idea, he edited leftover prose essays of his wife into books. He was not yet a lion among hostesses or the "champion diner-out of London"; but his literary popularity was burgeoning. Two volumes of Selections spread his reputation. And in 1864, publishing eighteen poems, half of them new, under the title Dramatis Personae, he had the happiness to find the book 'so well reviewed and so briskly purchased that it achieved a second edition within a single year.

Dramatis Personae contains six or eight of Browning's best-known poems, and about as many poems which the world has chosen to forget. The themes are more restricted than those of Men and Women, and there is a tighter system of argument and opinion. Renan, Strauss, Charles Darwin, and Thomas Huxley were having their say, and many of the poems of Dramatis Personae were worked or reworked with the idea of protecting conventional religious thought from such writers. Browning's style was hardening. Much versification is rough; much semantics is strained; much grammar is warped. The combination of welcome message and painful reading was no new thing for Browning, or for English poetry. It had been a favorite combination of John Donne, whom Browning admired in a day when Donne had few admirers. Carried to excess, as it often was in the poems of Dramatis Personae, it earned admonitory criticisms about "neglect of form." But Browning well understood the polemical utility of forcing interpretation upon the hearer; and workmanship, not neglect, produced his knotted affirmations of God, Hope, and the value of Struggle.

II *Male and Female*

Five of the poems in *Dramatis Personae* are about love relationships affected by marriage. In not a single case is a marriage
happy. Read as a group, the poems of erotic failure are tiring
as well as disheartening, for Browning unnecessarily used
them as vehicles for quiddities of language and reasoning.
The single poem which escapes such an arraignment is "Youth
and Art."

The most formidable of these poems about broken hearts
is "James Lee's Wife," or "James Lee," as the title stands
in the first edition. "James Lee's Wife" is actually nine separate
poems, each with its own title and its own distinctive verse
form. The setting of the first eight poems is the Normandy
coast, and of the ninth the ship which is to separate husband
and wife. Browning's speaker is the wife, and the successive
poems find her "At the Window," "By the Fireside," "In the
Doorway," "Along the Beach," "On the Cliff," "Reading a
Book, Under the Cliff," "Among the Rocks," "By the Drawing
Board," and, finally, "On Deck." The technical system of using
many poems of different metrical patterns to display a forward
movement and successive shifts of mood seems to reflect Tennyson's *Maud*, and the heavy ratiocination employed as overlay
to a simple story of failed marriage owes something to George
Meredith's sonnet-sequence *Modern Love*, a work then much
in the public eye.

Some stanzas of Browning's sixth poem, "Under the Cliff,"
had been printed in a periodical decades earlier.[2] They begin,
"Still ailing, wind? Wilt be appeased or no?" and it is possible
that, recurring to Browning in a spell of despondency and
bad weather, they served as the nuclear item of the long work.
The theme of the poem is genuine but overdeployed and
ultimately exhausting love. Browning himself summed up the
poem very neatly. "People newly married," he called the pair,
"trying to realize a dream of being sufficient to each other . . .
and finding it break up,—the man being *tired* first,—and tired
precisely of the love."[3] There are hints of special references
to the Browning menage in several of the subpoems, especially
in the eighth, "Beside the Drawing Board"; and Browning's
own hand underscored "tired" in the letter just quoted.

"The Worst of It," *"Dîs Aliter Visum,"* and "Too Late"

appeared in unbroken series in *Dramatis Personae*. Each of
them presents a love affair degenerated into falsehood,
cynicism, and despair. "The Worst of It" handles the fierce
lucubrations of a cuckolded husband towards his unfaithful
wife. Like other poems in the series, it is full of special pleading
and skewed logic. For example, in marrying a "speckled" person like himself, the lady had become so soiled as to move
naturally onward into adultery. As in "James Lee's Wife"
(though with sexes reversed), he allows that his adoration of
her may have contributed to her delinquency:

> I . . . tired
> Your soul, no doubt, till it sank! Unwise
> I loved and was lowly, loved and aspired,
> Loved, grovelling or glad, till I made you mad,
> And you meant to have hated or despised
> Whereas, you deceived me.

In spite of such reasonings, the man's self-pity and self-
righteousness are the emotions actually conveyed in this
unsatisfactory poem.

"*Dîs Aliter Visum*" bears the subtitle "Or, *Le Byron de Nos
Jours.*" In English the full title would be "The Gods Judge
Differently; or, The Byron of our Times." An artistic, sophisticated, and worldly man is in love with a very young girl,
and the girl admires and loves him in return. Foreseeing
incongruity and awkwardness for both partners in a May-
September marriage, the man does not propose. Now, ten years
later, he is married to a failing prima ballerina, and the girl
to a whist-playing nobody. The woman, who is the speaker,
calls her once-loved friend a fool and a coward. In deeming
the union imperfect, and in drawing back, the man has pre-
vented it from trying to perfect itself. In several stanzas,
Browning restates his theory that perfection equals death,
and that grappling with imperfection is a live man's proper
function:

> . . . what's whole can increase no more,
> Is dwarfed and dies, since here's its sphere.
> The devil laughed at you in his sleeve!
> You knew not? That I well believe;
> Or you had saved two souls: nay, four.

"Fool, for all/Your lore," she calls him. The first part of the title is now clear: the gods (like the woman) will scorn his "wisdom." The second part of this poem quietly mocks the sexual hesitations and manipulations of Browning's readers with the sexual gusto of Byron's. The speaker in "Too Late" has loved a girl, seen her marry another man, lived for six years in the belief that they can rejoin each other after all, and finally learned that the girl is dead. Browning conducts this man up and down the scale of passion and lets him vent his rage and despair in language of great vigor:

> There you stand [as hallucination]
> Warm too, and white too: would this wine
> Had washed all over that body of yours
> Ere I drink it, and you down with it: thus!

But the movements of this poem remain indistinct, and there is no clear line of progress.

"Youth and Art," the final poem of failed amours, compares to the others as Hyperion to a satyr. Utterly charming are the two young students, their serious studies, their cautious watching of each others' windows, their occasional burst of curiosity or jealousy, and, tragically, their failure ever to make a contact. Now, both married and enjoying their second-rate successes, they have time to contemplate what might have been:

> Each life unfulfilled, you see;
>   It hangs there, patchy and scrappy:
> We have not sighed deep, laughed free,
>   Starved, feasted, despaired,—been happy.
>
> And nobody calls you a dunce,
>   And people suppose me clever:
> This could but have happened once,
>   And we missed it, lost it for ever.

The language and system of thought employed by the speaker (the woman, this time) are of crystalline purity and strength. In its bittersweet humor and easy picturesqueness, its charm, grace, and masterful progression, "Youth and Art" was instantly popular and has always remained so.

III   *Whether God Is Dead*

Of the four poems of *Dramatis Personae* which most signifi-

cantly argue for the life and wisdom of God, the "Epilogue"
is least known. Its neglect is perhaps due to its unindicative
title, for it is a spirited and interesting piece. The other three
religious poems—"A Death in the Desert," "Rabbi ben Ezra,"
and "Caliban upon Setebos"—were the beneficiaries of a controversy very warm and trenchant in its day, though not so
much in ours.

The "Epilogue" to *Dramatis Personae* features three
speakers, one "as David," one "as Renan," and the third as
Browning himself. The "David" speaker chants a simple Old-
Testament situation: a whole culture, "swarming with one
accord," worships the actual presence of God in God's actual
Temple. The "Renan" speaker works with science, especially
the science of astronomy, and finds no Heaven and no Lord
in the star-filled sky. He sees no place "where may hide/What
came and loved our clay," and he cannot detect "the star which
chose to stoop and stay for us." Instead of a God, man finds
only himself the supreme being of the universe. Browning's
own voice, the third, tries to reconcile these two positions
of utter faith and utter doubt. His argument is metaphorical
and not especially easy to follow, but it winds up with the
clear statement that personal contact would not prove God,
or lack of it disprove God; and that nature (or science) and
God are equally present in the developed personality of man.

"Caliban upon Setebos" imagines religion as a savage might.
Caliban, the monster from Shakespeare's *Tempest*, sets forth
his beliefs from his own mouth. The God he worships, Setebos,
is made in his own image—he is contrarious, cruel, stupid,
and perhaps terrorized. Setebos's system of rule is through
torment: "He doth his worst in this our life,/Giving just respite
lest we die through pain,/Saving last pain for worst,—with
which an end." As he describes his god, Caliban illustrates
him by torturing helpless crabs or by feeding them—like
Setebos, he acts according to whims. But since he is low and
fearful, and since Setebos is like him, he must also imagine
a sort of super-God (whom he calls "the Quiet") towards whom
Setebos himself must be low and fearful. For this complex
but splendid poem, the most successful one of the religious
series, Browning provided a subtitle: "Natural Theology on
the Island." The danger warned against is that of anthropomor-
phism. If a highly developed intellectual (say Renan) may

construct a God with his own human traits, a loutish subhuman like Caliban may disastrously do the same.

Ben Ezra, the Rabbi whose harsh and angry "sermon on death" pleased the Jews of "Holy-Cross Day," delivers a more positive message in this poem that bears his name. "Rabbi ben Ezra" is best known by its opening stanza:

> Grow old along with me!
> The best is yet to be,
> The last of life, for which the first was made:
> Our times are in His hand
> Who said, "A whole I planned,
> Youth shows but half; trust God: see all nor be afraid."

Other stanzas maintain other favorite doctrines of the poet. The familiar doctrine that whatever is perfected has perished is carried all the way into the principle of faith. "A perfect faith" is the plaything of "fixed and finite clods." Weakness and sorrow are to be enjoyed, since they manifest man's vitality:

> Then welcome each rebuff
> That turns earth's smoothness rough,
> Each sting that bids nor sit nor stand, but go!
> Be our joys three-parts pain!
> Strive, and hold cheap the strain;
> Learn, nor account the pang; dare, never grudge the throe!

From this point the argument takes a long upward sweep, somewhat paralleling the development of the idea that the glad progress from youth to age is followed by a still gladder one from death to new life. The zest and enthusiasm of this poem are infectious, and may delight or inspire readers who do not in the least agree with the dogmatic contents.

"A Death in the Desert" purports to contain the dying words of St. John, "the beloved disciple," as recorded in a manuscript by a young Christian convert. There is a very intricate double framing of this final testament. The outermost part consists of bibliographical notations by persons who have owned the manuscript. Within that, magnificently detailed, are the place and circumstance: a cave in a desert mountainside and a handful of the starving faithful who try to protect John and themselves from the terrors of Christian martyrdom. John's farewell is the matter within the frames. Speaking in a lucid interval between senile coma and actual death, the apostle attempts to refute not only the errors of his own epoch but the heresies of the nineteenth century. Culminating his discourse is the argument that new increments of intelligence and learning among later generations will provide scope for new increments of religious knowledge and faith. The simple evidence of miracles will be replaced by the complex evidence of scientific knowledge. Man is built for continual development, and his religion may, or must, develop with his other accomplishments. As we have seen, this theme runs through all poems of the series.

IV   *The Fine Arts and Foul*

Browning's interest in poetic treatment of art and artists had somewhat diminished since the time of *Men and Women.* In earlier years he had used artistic subjects as screens between himself and his audience; now he was more ready to operate without the protection of screens. Compared to his earlier painter-poems, "A Face" and "A Likeness" are only scraps. "Abt Vogler," generally regarded as a masterpiece among his poems on music, was probably begun earlier, and owes its interest more to the philosophic side than to the musical side of its subject. Again written much earlier, perhaps in 1859, is "Mr. Sludge, the 'Medium'," a long blast against a spiritualistic practitioner whose art Browning did not like.

"A Face" and "A Likeness" are complementary. The first commemorates the extraordinary beauty of Amelia Patmore, wife of the poet Coventry Patmore, and was withheld from print until after her death in 1863. Its prettiest detail is the comparison of hyacinth buds against the lady's mouth to "angel faces" which "Corregio loved to mass, in rifts/Of Heaven." In "A Likeness," a man living alone possesses, with fifty other pictures, one likeness of an unknown girl:

> a print
> An etching, a mezzotint;
> 'Tis a study, a fancy, a fiction,
> Yet a fact (take my conviction)
> Because it has many a hint

> Of a certain face, I never
> Saw elsewhere, a touch or a trace of
> In women I've seen the face of.

He has in fact fallen in love with the print, and is depicted as waiting with mixed fear and eagerness for some friend to recognize the beauty as he has done. Two contrasting postulations have produced his anxiety. In one, as he thinks, a married man might love the picture except that a wife might be jealous of it; in the second, a young sportsman might love it except that his sporting friends might take no interest. In either case, the speaker's idol would be desecrated.

"Abt Vogler" presents a melange of music, psychology, philosophy, and religion—all intensified by the shifting passions of their spokesman. Vogler was a real musician of the eighteenth century. The poem introduces him just as he completes playing an improvisation on a small organ of nine hundred pipes, an "instrument of his own invention." In the exhilaration which follows the artistic act, he imagines his "notes" in context of great architecture, of crowds of artificers "eager to do and die," of the stellar cosmos, of great spirits yet to be born, and of "the wonderful Dead/Who have passed through their body and gone." Creative miracles can be wrought by "my music and me" and, as he generously concedes, by such other arts as painting and poetry. Man through art can frame "out of three sounds . . . not a fourth sound, but a star." This handsome image occurs among other images showing that imperfection (three sounds) on earth may translate to perfection (the star) in other worlds.

"Abt Vogler" is also of interest for biographical reasons. Vogler had become known to Browning very early, both through his writings and through the fact that Browning's music tutor, John Relfe, taught by the "system" which Vogler had developed.[4] The real Vogler's spotted reputation, his social ambiguity, and the allegations which had led to his being regarded alternately as a great genius and as a tinkling charlatan, undoubtedly added to Browning's interest. In "Mr. Sludge, the 'Medium'," the longest and probably the ugliest poem of *Dramatis Personae*, the elements of biographical and personal interest are stronger still. Browning had written most of this poem while Elizabeth Barrett was still alive, and had written it with the specific purpose of slurring her Spiritualist beliefs and the "medium" whom she trusted most.

The central target, D. D. Home, was an able, successful, ultimately wealthy man, whose clients were often crowned or tiara'd and who married into titled families not once but twice. Browning's poem takes Home, or Sludge, back to sordid days in Boston, and shows him abjectly begging for forgiveness and mercy from a rich American, Hiram H. Horsfall, his former sponsor who has just detected him to be a fraud. Browning's notions of how Americans speak and behave provide some instructive amusement: he makes both men more violent in their actions than similarly placed Britons would be, and he exceeds the likelihoods of their behavior with kneelings down (in supplication), kissing of hands (in gratitude), and stranglings (in anger, of course). The only intellectual interest in the poem arises from Sludge's self-exculpatory arguments, which take in the entire spectrum of human motivation. As is well known, Sludge partly excuses his cheating by claiming to believe partly in real spirits whom one may perhaps really contact. His other defenses are those which Lippi, Bloughram, and the others employ—his own needs, the needs of his clients, and sheer competitive reaction to the possibility that he will be outdone by his chief professional rival, "the Pennsylvania medium." That he is a worse human being than his duped clients he denies steadily, and perhaps successfully. But at the end of the poem, poor Sludge, his arguing all done, is shown falling into a childish tantrum and promising himself a set of childish revenges. The poem, brilliant enough up to then, is thus sacrificed to the personal hatred of Browning for Home.

V *Death*

The so-called "doctrine of the imperfect" has a manifest connection with conventional views of life after death. We live, love, and work imperfectly on this sphere; and the unwanted death which closes us out is the act of absolute imperfection. The line "What comes to perfection perishes" refers to perfection achieved in this life only. But suppose a God, suppose a heaven? Any process finished in those places might be perfect and might therefore cause problems.

Browning's most personal and least personal poems on death

equally embody this problem of the imperfect. "Prospice," his much-loved poem anticipating his feelings when he must come to die, will not stand very close analysis. The first half, or more, presents the speaker—certainly Browning—as a "hero," "a fighter," and a "strong man"; and shows that he is eligible for these titles because of his lack of dread of "the Arch Fear in a visible form." But all things inimical are denied in the closing lines:

> ... the elements' rage, the fiend-voices that rave,
>> Shall dwindle, shall blend,
> Shall change, shall become first a peace out of pain,
>> Then a light, then thy breast,
> Oh thou soul of my soul, I shall clasp thee again,
>> And with God be the rest!

If the end has been known, the vaunted courage has been mere common sense.

"Apparent Failure" is a finer poem on most counts, including its statement of the same doctrine. The occasion for the poem, namely a civic decision to tear down the "Doric little morgue" on the banks of the Seine River in Paris, became the occasion for a craggy reminiscence of visits paid to the place. Browning's stanzas on the interior—its fogged glass, jetting river-water, naked wet corpses, and drifting tourists—are a marvelous display of realism and point. Of the three corpses on display in the reminiscence, one is supposed to have been a socialist, one a royalist, and one a mere lecher:

> And this—why, he was red in vain,
>> Or black, poor fellow that is blue!
> What fancy was it turned your brain?
>> Oh, women were the prize for you!
> Money gets women, cards and dice
>> Get money, and ill-luck gets just
> The copper couch and one clear nice
>> Cool squirt of water o'er your bust,
> The right thing to extinguish lust!

In concluding, Browning mincingly parodies platitudes about being "good," "meek," and "fierce" in the voice of some more vulgar moralizer than he. His own conclusion reintroduces the paradox of imperfection in the world: God moves in a "wide compass round" to gather in these wet human fragments, and human condemnation is not in order.

"May and Death" and "Confessions" are companion poems. The first arose from the death of Browning's cousin James Silverthorne. Browning calls him "Charles" in the poem, and adds propriety to the passion of loss by somewhat feminizing the voice of the speaker. The poem focuses from large issues like love, death, and May to a single wild plant whose color and form express the heartbreak of the speaker. In "Confessions," a bolder effort by far, a dying man looks through the phalanx of medicine bottles on a bedroom table and sees the greatest scene of his life—a road, garden, terrace, and house where one June he has managed secret assignations with a girl who loved him. At the end, the reminiscence and the bottles actually coalesce—the girl

> ... left the attic there
> By the brim of the bottle labelled "Ether,"
> And stole from stair to stair.

The expiring speaker is relating this best of events to a clergyman who has come to hear his last confessions. He has none to make: his loving was "sad and bad and mad," but excused itself for him by being "sweet."

Browning believed firmly in the worth of his poem "Gold Hair," even going so far as to tinker and add to it in hopes of pleasing George Eliot, who "did not understand." His pride in it caused him to position it second in *Dramatis Personae*, right after the opus "James Lee's Wife." But neither the manner nor the narrative has won praise; and the appended "sermon," though purely Christian in context, has lead to a century of controversy. The narrative is simple and bold. A young girl of great purity and sweetness has but one treasure, a mass of hair—"such a wonder of flax and fless,/Freshness and Fragrance—flocks of it, too." Dying, still pure and virginal, she insists that her braids not be disturbed during the process of burial. Her goodness, coupled with the innocent vanity of her dying wishes, made her a saintly legend in her town of Pornic. But, after a few scores of years, when some work was being done on the church floor, a coin or two turned up:

> And lo, when they came to the coffin-lid

> Or rotten planks which composed it once,
> Why, there lay the girl's skull wedged amid
>   A mint of money, it served for the nonce
> To hold in its hair-heaps hid.

The "sermon" flatly charges the rationalistic naturalism of "Essays and Reviews" writers, and especially Bishop Colenso, with inability to explain the evil that lodges with good "in the human heart." For himself, Browning holds to the truth of the old faith for "reasons and reasons"—

> ... this, to begin,
> 'Tis the faith that launched point-blank her dart
>   At the head of a lie—taught Original Sin,
> The Corruption of Man's Heart.

Original sin does not imply the imposed damnation and eternal punishment of strict Calvinism; and there is no reason to say, as have DeVane and others, that the poem's "moral" is "perverse." "Gold Hair" way not convince, but within its premises it makes perfectly good sense.

CHAPTER 8

The Ring and the Book

I *Nine Years*

IN June, 1860, crossing "a square in Florence, crammed with
booths/Buzzing and blaze, noontime and market-time,"
Browning paused before a certain booth stocked with the
scraps and offal of Western culture—rockwork, broken busts,
faded scraps of ancient tapestry "now offered as a mat to save
bare feet." With the other rubbish were six books:

> A dog-eared Spicilegium, the old tale
> Of the Frail one of the Flower, by young Dumas,
> Vulgarized Horace for the use of schools,
> The Life, Death, Miracles of Saint Somebody,
> Saint Somebody else, his Miracles, Death, and Life,—
> With this, one glance at the lettered back of which,
> "Stall!" cried I: a lira made it mine. (I, 77-83)

The volume so purchased, called "The Old Yellow Book" in
English literature ever since, ran to two hundred and fifty
pages. The contents were some twenty-one documents and
letters about the unhappy marriage of a Roman girl, Pompilia
Comparini, and a minor nobleman of Arezzo, Count Guido
Franceschini; the culmination of this marriage in the murder
on January 2, 1698, of Pompilia; and the execution, scarcely
six weeks later, of Guido and the country louts he had chosen
to be his henchmen. Browning, who had long since shown
his love for a good murder, began reading the strange com-
posite volume as soon as it was his:

> Read I on, from written title-page
> To written index, on, through street and street,
> At the Strozzi, at the Pillar, at the Bridge;
> Till, by the time I stood at home again

> In Casa Guidi by Felice Church,
> Under the doorway where the black begins
> With the first stone-slab of the staircase cold
> I had mastered the contents, knew the whole truth,
> Gathered together, bound up in this book. (I, 110-18)

The "whole truth" Browning then compared to scraps of gold, but pure, unalloyed gold, useless for any purpose of creation. The major metaphor of the "ring," which balances the "book" in the poem, depends upon the alloyment of this gold by the addition of foreign substances—metals, heat, and baths of acid. The alloyment in this instance took place at night. The book, its raw gold now thoroughly transferred to the poet's mind, was placed upon a marble-top table, and the poet stepped out upon his terrace, contemplated the lighted-up church opposite, counted the people passing on the streets below, looked over the roofs and spires of Florence, and felt his consciousness be carried—

> A bowshot to the street's end, north away
> Out of the Roman gate to the Roman road,
> By the river, till I felt the Appenine.
> And there would lie Arezzo, the man's town
> The woman's trap and cage and torture place,
> Also the stage where the priest played his part,
> A spectacle for angels! (I, 498-504)

His own imagination became the alloying substance. The process was long, but the raw gold grew steadily harder and more suitable for use:

> This was it from, my fancy with true facts,
> I used to tell the tale, turning gay to grave,
> But lacked a listener seldom; such alloy
> Such substance of me interfused the gold
> Which, wrought into a shapely ring therewith,
> Hammered and filed, fingered and favored, last
> Lay ready for the renovating wash
> O' the water. (I, 679-86)

Much of the rest of Book One is a preliminary précis of the other books. Its conclusion, however, is the famous invocation

beginning "Oh lyric love, half angel and half bird," in which
Elizabeth Barrett is called from "the realms of help" to assist
in the writing. Gods, goddesses, or the Christian Divinity had
been invoked by the writers of epic-length poems from
Homer's time to Browning's; but Browning's wife-worship carried into the tactics of epic was a new departure within the
tradition.

Elizabeth had died less than a year after Browning's discovery, and apparently before his obsession about the Franceschini murders had jelled into resolution. The move to
London, the working out of a new way of life, and the reediting
of Elizabeth's work and his own, had kept him busy. But letters
of the years after 1861 are studded with references to his
"Roman murder story." Twice he offered the story to other
writers—a novelist and a historian—and several times he
engaged in minor researches, hoping to learn more about the
characters of the adventure. By the summer of 1864 he had
resolved to do the story himself, and on September 19, he
reported to Isa Blagden that the whole poem was "pretty well
in my head."[1] Within a few months, the writing was actually
under way. The usual accidents and blocks occurred, but the
work went steadily forward, usually at the rate of three hours
a day. In November, 1868, the first volume appeared, and
the second, third, and fourth were issued in the three succeeding months.

In Book One, Browning several times taunted his readers,
or nonreaders as he pretended, with the line "O British Public,
ye who love me not." As he knew, however, the British Public
had already come to rank him as one of its major poets, second
only to Tennyson. Consciously or subconsciously, he meant
to rise into parity with Tennyson. He meant *The Ring and
the Book* to be his *opus magnum*, the peak creation of his
life; and he meant for his genius to be measured by it at the
very time of its publication. This time, he had little disappointment, for reviewers and readers stood in close agreement
about the majesty of his creation. The critical comparers ranked
the book not only with Tennyson's best but with the best
of Spenser, Shakespeare, and Milton. Henceforth readers
might prefer Tennyson over Browning, but might also, without
causing amusement, prefer Browning over Tennyson. Now
there were two great Victorians.

II *Substance and Scheme*

The story which Browning read in the vellum-bound volume was in its essentials vulgar and uninspiring. It dealt with deceptions, greed, personal laxity, cruelty, despair, and finally murder. Carlyle called it a "mere Old Bailey case," worthy of no more than a half-column reportage; and there were plenty of others to share this view.

But it was an engrossing story. A middle-aged Roman couple, Pietro and Violante Comparini, had been living modestly on an inherited annuity which would stop with their deaths unless they themselves produced an heir. To keep the annuity from lapsing, Violante purchased the infant daughter of a Roman whore, deceived everyone, even her husband, into thinking it was her own child, named it Pompilia Comparini, and raised it to adolescence. Meanwhile, a decayed, ugly, and slow-witted minor nobleman, Count Guido Franceschini, lost his position as a Cardinal's hanger-on, and thought to improve his fortunes by marrying a woman of wealth. With the aid of his brother Paolo, a priest, he arranged a marriage with Pompilia. The wedding was garlanded with lies and deceptions on both sides. Pompilia, then "a tall girl of thirteen," was the only person in either menage who had no lies to tell; her lie was in her ancestry, which she did not yet know.

As part of the nuptial contracts, the Comparini had made over their possessions to Count Guido, who in turn engaged to support them as kin of nobility for the rest of their lives. Once in his rotting palace in Arezzo, however, they found themselves so chilled, starved, and insulted that a return to Rome was necessary. Safe back in Rome, and going to law to get the dowry back, Violante revealed that Pompilia was not her daughter but a drab's bastard. Much litigation resulted in the courts. Pompilia was still living in Arezzo as the wife of Guido, and the gradual building up of the lawsuit, plus the appalling fact that she was a penniless foundling and her husband was a cheated fool, earned increasingly cruel treatment for the innocent Pompilia. She sought help from the magistrates and from the local clergy, but without success. Finally, perhaps pregnant, and certainly filled with agony and fear, she obtained the help of a stylish young clergyman, the Canon Guiseppi Caponsacci. With him she eloped, as it were, towards Rome, where she planned to rejoin the Comparini.

Browning takes care to let their journey reflect journeys of Joseph and Mary and of the Brownings. The Pompilia-Caponsacci journey ended at an inn just outside Rome, where the couple stopped for a last night's rest. There Count Guido overtook them. There was some bedroom hocus-pocus and the threat of swordplay, terminating in the mundane imprisonment of the pair for adultery and the theft of the Franceschini jewelbox.

The wheels of the law rolled on. The verdict eventually was that Pompilia was Guido's legal wife but that, since she had never been a legal Comparini, neither she nor her spouse had any claim on the small wealth of that family. Guido's torment was now almost complete. His wife, though publicly branded as the spawn of a trull, remained his wedded wife; and he had lost not only her supposed fortune but his own chance to compete more successfully in the marriage market. Moreover, he was branded in Rome and Arezzo as a cuckold and laughing-stock. His breaking point came with the news that Pompilia was giving birth to a child whom he supposed to be Caponsacci's. All the years of pain and frustration now boiled over. Enlisting four young yokels of Arezzo to help him, he went to Rome, sulked through the Christmas season, got entry into the Comparini house, and stabbed the two false parents and their convalescing child to death. His escape was clumsily handled, and he and his boy-henchmen were caught, queried, tried, and executed in short order.

Browning imposed an exact form on this sprawling tale. Physically, *The Ring and the Book* echoes the epic tradition by having twelve separate parts. Ten of these are very extended dramatic monologues. Book One, "The Ring and the Book," has already been described; and Books Two, Three, and Four, entitled "Half-Rome," "The Other Half-Rome," and "Tertium Quid," constitute monologues by three citizens who justify (and in fact apotheosize) the dead Pompilia, justify and defend Count Guido, and take the cynical middle view that guilt and innocence are not the question. Books Eight and Nine, continuing the choric effect with an infusion of comedy, show the two lawyers Hyacynthus and Bottinius at work: the one is preparing an inept defense of the killer Guido; the other, a case for the prosecution, and both are bungling all the real issues while maintaining all the professional ones. Book

Twelve, "The Book and the Ring," by means of a series of accounts by witnesses, law students, and case collectors, draws the threads of action and opinion around to complete the circle. These seven books may be said to have told the story eight or nine times over, but, through sharp separation of the individual speakers, they have done this without repetition or overlapping. Grand as these books are, their function is to provide background for the five synoptic books of the poems, those uttered by Pompilia, Caponsacci, and the judging Pope, and by Count Guido, the single speaker who has two books in which to express his experience and comments.

III   *Roman Commentaries*

When Rome begins to speak, Pompilia, punctured by twenty-two stab wounds, "five mortal," is in a dying condition; Pietro and Violante are laid out for public view in the San Lorenzo church; Guido is in prison; and Caponsacci is still in his pleasant exile a few leagues outside the city.

Half-Rome, a creation which Browning personifies as a jealous husband, speaks cheerfully to an acquaintance about the relics in the church:

> Pietro the old murdered fool
> To the right of the altar, and his wretched wife
> On the other side. In trying to count stabs
> People supposed Violante showed the most
> Till somebody explained us that mistake;
> His wounds had been dealt out indifferent where,
> But she took all her stabbings in the face,
> Since punished thus solely for honor's sake,
> *Honoris causa,* that's the proper term. (II, 21-9)

He adds that "our gallants hold" it necessary to "disfigure subject, fray the face,/Not just take life and end, in clownish guise." This Half-Rome's attitude toward the dying Pompilia is equally scornful. He automatically judges Caponsacci to have been a cool adulterer:

> A priest—what else should the consoler be?
> With goodly shoulder blade and proper leg,
> A portly make and a symmetric shape,
> And curls that clustered to the tonsure quite ...
>
> .   .   .   .   .   .

> Apollos turned Apollo, while the snake
> Pompilia writhed transfixed.   (II, 784-95)

Though despising Guido's ineffectiveness and procrastination,
Half-Rome sees Guido as the abused person; and, in his re-
hearsal of the lawcase about dowry, divorce, and legitimacy,
he unceasingly shows how Guido has been bilked. He is most
caustic of all about Pompilia's child. First he imagines the
love-affair as continuing, with "some muffled Caponsacci"
going to her to "employ odd moments." Then—

> Pompilia—what? sang, danced, saw company?
> —Gave birth, sir, to a child, his son and heir,
> Or Guido's heir and Caponsacci's son.   (II, 1382-84)

No wonder, says Half-Rome, that Guido cracked: "The over-
burdened mind/Broke down, what was a brain became a
blaze." In collecting his four "hard hands and stout hearts
/From field and farrow," and in going to Rome for the blood-
feast, Guido was doing only what he had to do.

Half-Rome's cruelties of speech and wish are too pat as the
result of his own sexual jealousy, and he closes by sending
a warning to "a certain what's his name and jackanapes
/Somewhat too civil of eves with lute and song/About a house
here, where I keep my wife." The speaker in "The Other
Half-Rome" begins on an ethical, or even a credulous note.
At first, his thoughts are locked on Pompilia, who lies dying
in "the long white lazar-house." He accepts the possibility
that Pompilia may be a saint, divinely saved from her twenty-
two wounds, "five mortal," until her hagiographical story may
be told.

> ... really it does not seem as if she here,
> Pompilia, living so and dying thus,
> Has had undue experience how much crime
> A heart can hatch. Why was she made to learn ...
> What Guido Franceschini's heart could hold?
> Thus saintship is effected probably;
> Not sparing saints the process! (III, 105-12)

As he retells the saint's story, Other Half-Rome keys all events
to Guido's evil and Pompilia's goodness. Caponsacci he

automatically clears of wrongdoing. The Comparini are not
ethical subjects, only "a beaten brace of stupid dupes." More
than the other speakers, Other Half-Rome opens his discourse
to a lot of invented monologues by other speakers, most of
whom speak later in their own books. But eventually his bland
mask slips: at the very end of the poem, Browning reveals
him as not merely half of Rome but as a disappointed business
connection of the Franceschini. Guido's family has injured
him long ago, and he recalls—

> The lie that was, as it were, imputed me
> When you objected to my contract's clause,—
> The theft as good as, as may say, alleged
> When you, co-heir in a will, excepted, Sir,
> To my administration of effects. (III, 1684-88)

Thus each general judgment is merely a front for a personal
bias. Altick and Louks, in their excellent book *Browning's
Roman Murder Story*, argue that the neutrality and objectivity
often attributed to Tertium Quid is really a "thoroughgoing
partisanship" for Count Guido.[2] Persons who read Book Four
with care will find not so much partisanship for Guido as a
failure of ethical partisanship of any kind. The disputed intentions of Caponsacci—that is, to save Pompilia or to sleep with
her—are both acceptable to Tertium Quid; indeed, he finds
both ideas amusing. No simpleton about cruelty or bad motives,
he is the first to suggest squarely that the torments Guido
perhaps visited upon Pompilia were blows at the two Comparini:

> How reach at them?
> Two hateful faces, grinning all aglow,
> Not only make parade of spoil they filched
> But foul him from the height of a tower, you see.
> Unluckily temptation is at hand—
> To take revenge on a trifle overlooked,
> A pet lamb they have left in reach outside,
> Whose first bleat, when he plucks the wool away,
> Will strike the grinners grave: his wife remains.(IV, 659-68)

But Guido was attempting, thinks Tertium Quid, a still harder
blow. Can he "drive herself to plague herself—/Herself disgrace herself and so disgrace/Who seek to disgrace Guido?"

If mistreated enough, that is, Pompilia would be driven to run off with another man; and Guido would have the sanction to do what he liked. Tertium Quid, however, has nothing judgmental to say about such a plan; for his natural metaphors for human activities are beast activities. Culmination of this tendency occurs in the murder scene when Guido is compared to a bull driven so mad with pain as to attack everyone in reach. "D'you blame the bull?" Tertium Quid asks reasonably.

The two lawyers Hyacinthus and Bottinius display ethical lapses of a different sort. The three lay-critics have had axes to grind, and each has externalized a need of his own as he rehearsed the case. Neither lawyer is that involved. Hyacinthus, the defender of Guido, is a lover of home and family, "home-joy, the family board,/Altar and hearth." All these are focused at the moment upon an eight-year-old son, a promising and affectionate lad whom the adoring Hyacinthus can hardly bear to send from the room as he begins to write his case. A problem case, of course. Guido has confessed, would be known as the killer anyway, and is neither admired nor loved. Since nothing is to be said for Guido himself, Hyacinthus goes directly to concepts. His series of arguments employs a whole armory of principles and analogies (usually false) drawn from Persian, Hebrew, Greek, Roman, "human," and "natural" laws concerning crime and punishment. Semantic shifts help also; "murder," for example, is subtly changed, on two occasions, to "an abnormal act" and "secular business." Within his relaxed limits, Hyacinthus does his professional best to prepare a good case for his client, but he is still a relaxed family man. Among his first and last remarks are these:

> So, Liver fizz, law flit, and Latin fly,
> As we rub hands o'er dish by way of grace.
> .   .   .   .
> Into the pigeon-hole with thee, my speech!
> Off and away, first work, then play, play, play.

Bottinius, whom Hyacinthus calls a "beast," and whose celibacy and strictness he despises, calls Hyacinthus a "fat fool" and suggests that his "feeding hath offuscated his wit." Bottinius's strategies as prosecuting attorney depend less on the quirks and oddities of law than had Hyacinthus's. His attack on Guido is made swiftly and then abandoned; for, as he reasons, the Court is tired of hearing about Guido. Pompilia is another matter: he can excite them with the youth, the sufferings, and the hinted lecheries of Pompilia. By gradual development, then, he shows Pompilia in progressively more interesting situations—animalistic, resentful, romantic, tortured, humiliated, and carried away by her priest, who (as Bottinius gladly allows) may easily have seduced or assaulted her. His "painting sainthood" is only to "depicture sin." Like Hyacinthus, he is daring; and, on one occasion, he even compares Pompilia's pregnancy to the Immaculate Conception: "Someone must be sire:/And who shall say, in such a puzzling strait,/If there were not vouchsafed some miracle?" From this apex of unreason Bottinius descends gradually through suggestions, expressed through questions, of some minor miracles perhaps attributable to Pompilia, and to a quite calm conclusion that a pretty-girl saint has been destroyed by an ugly devil. His last words indicate his merely workmanlike view of the saintly aspect he has presented:

> There's my oration—much exceeds in length
> That famed panegyric of Isocrates.
> They say it took him fifteen years to pen.
> But all those ancients could say anything!
> He put in just what rushed into his head,
> While I shall have to prune and pare and print.
> This comes of being born in modern times
> With priests for auditory. Still, it pays.

Neither he nor Hyacinthus has had opinions or feelings to register, and neither would have found any difficulty in taking the opposite side if retained to do so.

IV *The Virtuous*

The three people who alone exemplify virtue in *The Ring and the Book* are Pompilia, Caponsacci, and Pope Innocent the Twelfth who, as leader of the Roman state, had to make the final decisions about Count Guido and his henchmen. Browning's admiration for Pompilia had been developing into a bona-fide Victorian girl-worship as he lived year after year with the idea of her troubles. In providing her with a Caponsacci of his own invention, and finally with the loving but judgmental Pope, he was giving her a lover and a father. He also gave her a religious status, and makes the Papal lawyer Archangelis describe her as "faultless to a fault." A Catholic writer in the *Dublin Review*, while admiring the poem in general, found her knight and savior Caponsacci "too like a young English parson" to fit the occasion.[3] The Pope's own monologue is discursive and socially competent. Its main interest, perhaps, is its one-for-one relationship with Browning's own thinking about virtue, church, and civilization. Its judgments of guilt and innocence are absolute, and may seem dogmatic today.

Raised by elderly idiots, married at thirteen, sequestered for four years in a mouldering provincial palazzo, and slaughtered in her seventeenth year, Pompilia represents waste and misuse of good objects. Her monologue takes place in her final hours. Lying "in hospital white," she speculates on the fate, not of herself first, but of her two-week-old son:

> Now I shall never see him; what is worse
> When he grows up and gets to be my age
> He will seem hardly more than a great boy;
> And if he asks, "What was my mother like?"
> Someone may answer, "Like girls of seventeen"—
> And how can he but think of this and that,
> Lucias, Marias, Sofias, who titter and blush
> When he regards them as such boys may do?" (VII, 64-71)

The rest of her discourse, so far as she speaks of herself, maintains the same self-observing and fondling terms. She is sharper at other times. She has had childhood dreams of a lovely young cavalier—

> ... he proved Guido Franceschini,—old
> And nothing like so tall as I myself,
> Hook-nosed and yellow in a bush of beard,
> Much like a thing I saw on a boy's wrist,
> He called an owl and used for catching birds.
>   (VII, 394-98)

Now that Guido has killed her, she pardons him, in a way. But her judgments continue, and indeed rise into emotional tropes and tricks of logic that ill match her character. Since she was the source of Guido's hate, she trusts, for example, that her permanent "evanishment" may "help further to relieve the heart that cast/Such object of its natural loathing forth."

The cavalier that Pompilia had dreamed of as a little girl has turned out to be Canon Caponsacci. She admits to loving this man, though in a fleshless way compatible with the vows both have taken. Dying and absent from him, she is still with him:

> Oh lover of my life, Oh soldier saint,
> No work begun shall ever pause for death!
> Love will be helpful to me more and more
> In the coming course, the new path I must tread—
> My weak hand in thy strong hand, strong for that!
>
> (VII, 1786-90)

It has been a matter of remark to all parties that the Canon is young, vigorous, given to hand-holding and flirtation. He claims to have become a priest by error, or actually by seduction, since the Bishop who ordained him has promised that he need not give up his worldly pleasures in the service of God. Caponsacci's vows, then, have made him only a fashionable and womanizing priest, a cassocked Squire of Dames, as he admits. He denies, however, that his relationship with Pompilia was self-generated. Guido and a kinsman, he argues in court, have hoped to manipulate Pompilia into adultery through contriving the meeting. To the harder question of whether there was anything special, that is, beyond his Christian responsibilities, about his love for Pompilia, he answers a violent yes:

> I apprise you...
> That I assuredly did bow, was blessed,
> By the revelation of Pompilia. There!
> Such is the final fact I fling you, Sirs,
> To mouth and mumble and misinterpret: there!
> "The Priest's in love," have it the vulgar way!
> Unpriest me, rend the rags of the vestment, do—
> Degrade me, disenfranchise all you dare—
> Remove me from thy midst, no longer priest
> And fit companion. (VI, 1864-72)

By this time one of the judges is weeping. That "the priest's in love" turns out acceptable to this court and later to the Pope. The saintliness of Pompilia is, as Browning would have it, the clear guarantee that nothing is wrong. "For Pompilia," the Canon sums up, "build churches, go pray."

Browning's Pope Innocent the Twelfth has been much praised for the mature philosophy and morality he has been supposed to utter, but a less charitable view towards him is possible. For one thing, he speaks of himself and his responsibilities at too great a length—fully a third of his Book. Browning makes use of him to argue the great nineteenth-century question of papal infallibility, and reaches the conclusion (contrary to the nineteenth-century Catholic Church) that Popes are men and not infallible. Innocent's other opinions are of the same adamancy but not the same modesty, and his judgments are extreme and rigid. Pompilia, housed during childhood with the morally muddled Comparini, has been the builder of her own sanctity, therefore the Pope finds her doubly sainted. And Guido, having trained and worked in Church settings, is, with the same reasoning, doubly devilized. The Pope is more interesting when he leaves his loved-or-loathed individual subjects and turns to a general evaluation of the churchly and religious premises upon which he claims to have tried to base his verdicts. Church law he abandons very quickly; the Church has lost Christ: "The mystic Spouse betrays the Bridegroom here." Since general religion is moving towards faith in mere science and reason, the mission of the age is to shake "the torpor of assurance" from Christianity, and to "Re-introduce the doubt discarded, bring/That formidable danger back, we drove/Long ago to the distance and the dark." For now, the future of the Christian civilization depends on the mere feelings of individuals:

> [Perhaps] some one Pompilia left [to] the world
> Will say, "I know the right place by foot's feel,
> I took it and tread firm there; wherefore change?"
> But what a multitude will surely fall
> Quite through the crumbling truth, late subjacent,
> Sink to the next discoverable base,
> Rest upon human nature, settle there
> On what is firm, the lust and pride of life!
> A mass of men, whose very souls even now
> Seem to need recreating,—so they slink
> Wormlike into the mud. (X, 1885-95)

The hope is in a "new law," superseding the Christian one and the Jewish one. The successor to Moses and Jesus might be—and why not?—merely the little Pompilia.

V *Count Guido*

Considered either as a historical reconstruction or as a dramatic invention, Count Guido Franceschini is the most thoroughly reported man in all of Browning's works. He may also strike readers as the most interesting, but the interest must arise because of his common rather than his uncommon qualities. Contrary to what some other speakers say, it is not greed, sadism, or vengefulness which distinguish his character. His fault is meanness, skimpiness, human inadequacy. His tragedy, which spreads out to cover so many other individuals, is mere failure of a small man to cope with large problems.

Inadequacy marks even his face and form. Short, small-boned, ugly, dull-eyed and droopy-mouthed, "past his prime of life, and out of health," Guido has nothing to support his self-esteem but an old name and rank, both of them "secondary." Above all, he lacks initiative. Aristotle reminds us to sketch men by their deeds rather than words. In deeds, Guido is continually the puppet and vehicle, a man acted upon rather than acting. His controllers vary widely—mother, brother, Violante, Court, Pope, public executioners—but one or another is in every case the moving force of his sanely conducted acts. Left to himself, as when he takes to tormenting Pompilia or when he seeks her out to kill her, he acts stupidly and suicidally. To him, autonomy means irrationality and death.

This ignoble Count compensates for his weakness in action with great power in talk. Some of Guido's statements are sharp. He can insult the very court that is trying him, and he mocks the Christian dignitaries who offer him comfort on his last day. But he is most eloquent on the subject of his rights and responsibilities. As a Count and the heir of an ancient name, he fills the air with claims of his obligations. His murder of Pompilia and the Comparini was, if rightly construed, a civic obligation:

> Absolve me, then, law's mere executant!
> Protect your own defender. . . .

> It would be too fond, too complacent, play
> Into the hands of the devil, should we lose
> The game here, I for God: a soldier-bee
> That yields his life, extenerate with the stroke
> Of the sting that saves the hive. (V, 2003-11)

Browning lets such talk be contradicted by Guido himself in other arguments, for the Guido who cannot support his own autonomy cannot support social morality. "There was no way of making Guido great," as Tertium Quid rightly says.

In modern medicine, Guido would be labeled an asthenic and psychopath, a man born for failure, but also born for agony. For such a man every decision and every act entail prior feelings of fear and distrust, and subsequent feelings of guilt and despair. In Guido's uniquely doubled monologues we may watch him trip, and slip, and curve around such feelings. Violante can cheat him, Pietro can join in, even the teenage innocent Pompilia is more than a match for him, not to mention Caponsacci—and, in fact, everyone. His every effort is made in desperation, and results in some still greater desperation. And all the pain is locked within him, unshared and undispersed, for neither he nor his. pain is taken seriously, and where another man might get sympathy and support he gets only laughter. Shriveling with inner pain, Guido earns only "town talk ... square's jest, street's jeer."

Guido is always unable to conceive of his acts as sinful. Being the modern man the Pope takes him for, indeed, he asks the great question of the cause of his being what he is:

> Oh how I wish some cold wise man
> Would dig beneath the surface which you scrape;
> Deal with the depths, pronounce on my deserts
> Groundedly! I want simple sober sense,
> That asks before it finishes with a dog,
> Who taught the dog the trick you hang him for. (XI, 946-51)

He has not made himself; he does not rule himself; for, as we have seen, he is led and controlled, and always to his own cost. Deprived of his leaders and controllers, he loses not only his direction but his sanity. There is no reason to doubt his description of near-blackout suffered as he led his four young idiots towards Rome and vengeance:

> ... Out we flung and on we ran or reeled
> Romeward. I have no memory of our way,
> Only that, when at intervals the cloud
> Of horror about me opened to let in life,
> I listened to some song in the ear, some snatch
> Of a legend, relic of religion ...
> Then the cloud re-emcompassed me. (V, 1567-78)

His nine-day pause after reaching the city, a pause sometimes laid to its being Christmastide, was actually caused by a failure of both mind and will; and the murder which terminated the pause was the final snapping of a nervous tension too great to bear.

Such a man, incapable of soberly autonomous decision, plays to lose as often as he plays to win. It must be noticed that Guido manages to build virtual suicide into his murders. Several speakers, including the supposedly wise Pope, find it inexplicable that he did not prepare a retreat. A permit or exit visa was required before post-horses could be obtained, and Guido, though "a resident of Rome for thirty years," neglected to apply for one. The Pope rather chortlingly explains this error as mere negligence: "One touch of fool in Guido the astute!" No modern reader should follow the Pope in this judgment. The omission had to be deliberate, though not necessarily conscious. One of the mechanisms that would come into play is the simple craving for punishment which guilty people so often manifest. Another is the desire to have an end to fifty years of failure. Most of all, Guido needed to have a triumph at last; and it would come with celebrated victories in the Roman courts and with his acceptance as the champion of Christian morality which, at least in his first monologue, he repeatedly claims to be. The element of confusion in these motivations would perfectly suit the confused and, as I believe, pitiable character of Guido.

CHAPTER 9

Browning and the Classics

I *Why Hunt Hellenes?*

B ROWNING'S poem "Development," with its signifi-cant beginning, "My father was a scholar, and knew Greek," was still to be written. Browning's own interest in Greek had been displayed from time to time through "Artemis Prologuizes" and other poems. He had also had the advantage of living with Elizabeth Barrett, whose Classical knowledge appears to have been greater than his own. And from about 1864 onward he was deeply concerned about the academic career of his son, Penini, whose ill-met responsibilities included a working knowledge of the ancient languages and literatures. Thus there was a network of family reasons for the Classical studies into which Browning now threw himself. And there were other reasons, one of them rooted in Brow-ning's friendships, and one in the reactive professionalism of an artist unwilling to go too far in a single direction.

The friends were the Countess Cowper, a society hostess of good intellect and reading; Thomas Carlyle, now one of Browning's most revered old friends; and Benjamin Jowett, then Senior Tutor at Balliol College and one of the most influential educators of Victorian Britain. Lady Cowper's mem-ory hardly survives except in Browning's dedication to *Balaus-tion's Adventure* in which she is said to have "the Greek qual-ities of goodness and beauty" and is charged with imposing upon him the task of doing the poem. Carlyle, perhaps as a joke, repeatedly went on record as suggesting that Browning's true vocation was in translating other men's poems. Jowett's name haunts the whole history of Victorian intellectualism. A Classical master, sometimes a historian, he was the most revered don of the most celebrated college of Oxford. Browning had sought his friendship with the deliberate intention of advancing the college career of Penini. Much more than

Penini, he himself came under the spell of Jowett. They were
to remain friends for life, but hardly equal friends, since Browning was always content to sit "under" Jowett, while Jowett
was the proud type of schoolmaster who sits under no man.

Besides the conscious or unconscious pressures exerted by
such persons, Browning had his own image and self-image
to consider. The classical years of 1871–1877—when the volumes *Balaustion's Adventure, Aristophanes' Apology*, and the
Agamemnon of Aeschylus were published—were also the
years in which *Prince Hohenstiel-Schwangau, Fifine at the
Fair, Red-Cotton Night-cap Country*, and *The Inn Album* went
forth, all of them ugly, painful, controversial—sharply non-
classic. If Balaustion speaks for Browning, as she certainly
speaks for Elizabeth Barrett, the Classic modes were so high,
pure, and correct as to pay for modes on the other side of reality;
and Browning's part-time devotion to Hellenism was the
justifying obverse of his devotion to the grotesque.

II *Balaustion's Adventure*

"Balaustion" means wild pomegranate, and Browning's
selection of this name for the heroine of volumes concerned
with the Greeks pleasantly reminds readers of the "Bells and
Pomegranates Series" of thirty years before. The full name
of the first Balaustion volume is *Balaustion's Adventure,
including a Transcript from Euripides*. The "adventure"
serves as frame to the "transcript"—or in regular English, the
"translation"—of the *Alkestes* of Euripides. During the
Peloponnesian wars, the Athens-oriented city of Rhodes
shifted its allegiance to the Spartan League. In the poem, however, certain citizens of Rhodes whose Athenian sympathies
continue strong find an unlikely leader in the fourteen-year-old
Balaustion. Balaustion has a particular interest in Athenian
drama—"the great Dionysian theatre,/And tragic triad of
immortal fames,/Aeschules, Sophokles, Euripides!" All Rho-
dians who "have a soul," she cries, will honor these men,
reject the Spartan alliance, and go with her to Athens.

Though Balaustion was Browning's creation, her adventure
is based on a passage from Plutarch's *Lives*.[1] According to
Plutarch, the Sparta-oriented Syracusans enslaved and mistreated Athenian sympathizers who fell into their hands; but

the enslavers were so fascinated by the speedily grown reputation of Euripides, the "third tragic poet," as to give special favor to persons who could quote a little of his work. Balaustion and her shipmates, pursued by pirates and trying to take refuge in a Sicilian port, are refused entry and refuge by a Syracusan patrol galley. Fortunately, one of the patrol officers hears Balaustion encouraging her rowers with a song from a play by Aeschylus and inquires about Euripides, "the newer and not yet so famous bard." Balaustion, who knows "from first to last/That strangest, saddest, sweetest song of his, /ALKESTIS," is able to get help for her whole party by reciting it. As a bonus, she is noticed and loved by a young Syracusan, Euthukles, who is attracted by her recitations and follows her on board. This pair, one more of Browning's elopement pairs, is married upon arrival in Athens.

Topical reasoning may also have influenced Browning's choice of the *Alkestis* of Euripides for translation. The original Alkestis was wife to Admetos, King of Thessaly. As part of some larger transactions among the gods, Admetos is doomed to die unless some friend will volunteer to die in his place. No outside volunteers having appeared, Alkestes offers herself as the surrogate victim. Her single demand is for the about-to-be bereaved Admetos to swear never to marry again, and we recall the vows promised in "Any Wife to Any Husband" and other marital poems of Browning—vows quite likely exacted by Elizabeth Barrett herself. Euripides had been Elizabeth Barrett's favorite tragic playwright, and Browning not only used her quatrain about "Euripides the human/With his droppings of warm tears" as an epigraph to *Balaustion's Adventure,* but also caused Balaustion to claim personal aquaintance with a poetess who, "among her glories that will never fade," alone developed that perfect "style and title for Euripides."

Finally, we may suspect that in his half-praise, but also half-defense, of a Greek poet regarded as daring, individualistic, and perhaps decadent, Browning thought or felt something of the world's comparisons between himself and the more traditionalistic and stately Tennyson. A "thin critic" points out at the end that Euripides had "failed to get the prize . . ./Sophocles got it!" Balaustion answers correctly that "All cannot love two great names, yet some do." England just then possessed only two poets regarded as great, and it is difficult not to see this exchange as an allusion to the debate about poetic supremacy which had begun upon publication of *The Ring and the Book* only two years earlier.

III   Aristophanes' Apology

Balaustion's Adventure was published in August, 1871, and good sales led to a new edition in 1872. This work was followed by *Prince Hohenstiel-Schwangau* (1871), *Fifine at the Fair* (1872), and *Red-Cotton Nightcap Country* (1873)—all set in modern times and all calculated to set on edge the teeth of the readers who had so admired *The Ring and the Book*. In turn, these publications were followed by *Aristophanes' Apology* (1875) in which the Rhodian girl—or now, Athenian woman—much more heavily offers a second translation from Euripides. Next to *The Ring and the Book, Aristophanes' Apology* is Browning's longest poem; and in every other respect—scholarship, critical dicta, logical analysis, diffusion of language—it places the severest demands upon its reader.

The play recited this time is the *Hercules Furens*, or Mad Hercules. In Euripides's straightforward retelling of a simple anecdote from myth, Hercules returns from the twelfth and hardest of his labors to find his children, wife, and ancient father on the point of being killed by Lukos, King of Cadmus. He kills Lukos instead; but then, exhausted and in a paranoiac frenzy, he completes Lukos's work by slaughtering his own family. This gruesome play is set by Browning within two separate frames. The outermost one is another sea adventure, the flight of Balaustion and her husband Euthukles from Athens, which has just sustained its final defeat by the Spartan League. Within this frame, and told at much greater length, is an all-night dialogue at the house of Balaustion in Athens, the principal debaters being Balaustion and Aristophanes the comic playwright. The play of *Hercules Furens*, occurring within these nested frames, is recited by Balaustion as illustrative of her critical views. Scrupulously or not, Browning made the volume a carryall vehicle for his erudition about the subject of Greek life and letters. Though "priceless to the student," wrote J. A. Symonds in an otherwise approving review, the crushing burden of fact and allusion "will repel the general reader."[2] In our time, few people can read the book to its end.

As already suggested, *Aristophanes' Apology* partly reflects the growing concern of Browning towards lines of criticism that were being taken towards his own volume-length narratives. Some two thousand lines of the poem are devoted to critical adamancies in which Balaustion defends such modern, cool-headed, ethically aloof strategies as those followed by Euripides; and Aristophanes defends gutty, deeply involved, socially responsible strategies such as those followed by himself. As we would expect, Balaustion is concerned with the ribaldry and "ordure" to be found in Athenian comedy, and Aristophanes defends them as social instruments of irreplaceable value. When a recurring dispute occurs on the question of what audience is to be pleased, Balaustion argues that one should write for the cultivated; Aristophanes, that one should write for the democratic masses.

Of all the disputes, the most important concerns the responsibilities of creative satirists to their communities and cultures. Balaustion has only apprehended admonitory humor in a general way:

> This then is Comedy, our sacred song,
> Censor of vice, and virtue's guard as sure:
> Manners-instructing, morals' stop-estray,
> Which, born a twin with public liberty,
> Thrives with its welfare, dwindles with its wane. (3271)

Aristophanes with much more sophistication shows the essentially conservative and popular bearings of satire. He espouses "achieved truth," old "laws and customs," and "solid vulgar life." In his opinion, analytical and dispassionate storytelling such as that attributed to Euripides demonstrated not only social isolation but civic irresponsibility as well. The end result would be pride, sophistry, skepticism, and moral anarchy—the very Athenian weaknesses which were to deliver all Greece into the hands of Sparta.

As Sir Frederic Kenyon has indicated, there can never be a victor in such an argument. The problems at issue are "of conflicting tastes, of different ideas and aims, a clash, not of good with evil, but of good with good."[3] Within the book, Browning's Balaustion and Aristophanes conclude in mutual affection; and the former is made to envisage a "cleansed" fusion of tragedy and comedy: "Some new Both-yet-neither, all one bard/Euripides with Aristophanes/Cooperant!" Meanwhile, neither the intellectual Euripides nor the dirt-slinging Aristophanes was saving Athens; but, if either had, it would have been the tragic poet. Using Plutarch again, Browning tells how the Spartan commander Lysander, who had decreed the physical destruction of the great city, countermanded the orders after hearing some especially noble passage from Euripides. The argument from that circumstance would be that the supposedly unpolitical man may, after all, be the most successful public benefactor.

IV   The Agamemnon of Aeschylus, *and Out*

The second adventure of Balaustion was less acceptable to Browning's audience than the first one had been, and no second printing was required. Lady Cowper was not involved this time. Carlyle's responses were mixed and contradictory; he disliked the roundabout apparatus of the frames, but thought that a "vocation" showed in the inset translation of *Hercules Furens*. Jowett may not have approved of the book, and Browning may have felt squeezed in when "half a dozen critics reported the poem to be the *transcript*" of Jowett's talk.[4] His boyhood friend Domett, with other people, called for footnotes which might help to explain his thousand obscure allusions.[5] Browning rejected all such opinions and suggestions, but the edginess with which the poem had been received had somewhat shaken him.

To *The Agamemnon of Aeschylus* (1877), the last of his Greek books, Browning added a prose preface of unusual solicitude. Two things, he admitted, might need some explaining. One was the stylistic ruggedness of the verse in his translation, the other his unique spellings of Greek names. A few lines will illustrate the first matter, style:

> HERALD: Ha, my forefathers' soil of earth Argeian!
>   Thee, in this year's tenth light, am I returned to—
>   Of many broken hopes, on one hope chancing;
>   For never prayed I, in this earth Argeian
>   Dying, to share my part in tomb the dearest. (527-31)

The needless lack of grace and clarity in such lines was

explained by Browning as the product of his aim "to be literal at every cost save that of absolute violence to language." Nor, he continued, must he work for clarity of thought, since even Greeks admitted finding Aeschylus "hard to understand." Where Aeschylus had made no sense, Browning felt no need to make sense. As to his spellings of proper names, he had now (and in other works running back three decades) resolutely spelled "Greek names and places just as does the Greek author." Among the unhappy results were "Klutainmestra," "Threkian," "Skulla"—though these and other variations neglect the fact that the Greeks had never pronounced their letters as modern anglophones do.

Briefly, Browning had in both proceedings violated the principle that to attempt literal substitutions between unlike languages must inevitably produce a monster-tongue possessing the character of neither. "Threkia" shocks an anglophone no less than "Thrace" would have shocked a Greek; and the fact that the Greek would know a combining term does not absolve "avenging-ghost," used for "avenging ghost," from being nonword and nongrammar. His attempt to reproduce Greek hexameters led him to invent a halting, hesitating, often tangling meter of eleven syllables per verse. Because of his unfaltering literalism, he was unable to form or emphasize traits of the dramatis personae as many translators may do. All characters speak in the hard-bound style and tiring meter of the Herald, all sound much alike, and all are easily dismissed when the play is over. Hurt readers rebel. Carlyle, to whom the third Greek volume was dedicated, rendered an ultimate verdict of "very foolish." Algernon Swinburne, whose opinion is especially important because of his intimacy with Jowett, called the work "beyond belief—or caricature."[6] Penini Browning was meanwhile failing in his own problems with the Classics. The friendship between the poet and the Master of Balliol continued, but the poet's son was dropped from the college and a little later from the university.

CHAPTER 10

Four Tales of the Under Side

I The Route from Morbid to Horrible

REVIEWING *Balaustion's Adventure* for *The Nation* in 1871, J. R. Dennett commented that Browning was "always pleased to take a story where ninety nine story-tellers would leave it, or have left it, and turn it over and over, and peer into it, and lay bare all the intricate filaments of motive." Though not yet a cult figure, Browning was then at the height of his popularity among the actual reading public. His *Poetical Works*, published less than three years earlier, was going into repeated impressions. By purchase or piracy, he was widely printed in America and other countries. *The Ring and the Book* was still the wonder of readers and reviewers; and *Balaustion's Adventure*, even the Euripides in it, was innocent and Attick. But Dennett, looking at the characteristics of Browning's work up to 1871, also had an eye to what was to come. Browning's view of mankind, he wrote, was "of a subtlety that makes him almost a demonstration of morbid psychology."[1] And such was the course which from 1871 to 1875 Browning's genius was increasingly to follow.

Browning's outward life in these years was tranquil and easy. He had made the error, in 1869, of proposing marriage to Louisa, Lady Ashburton, a dashing millionairess widow who was his hostess on a long vacation in Scotland, and outrageously informing her that the marriage would be for his son's sake since his own heart "lay buried in Florence." Thenceforward, though he maintained intimate relationships with many women, he kept the idea of marriage at arm's length. In other ways he prospered. From his base on Warwick Crescent he embarked on periodic travels, his sister Sariana usually accompanying him to look after details. He saw a good deal of his old friend, almost his discoverer, the French critic Joseph Milsand. And, at the beginning of 1872, when his oldest and dearest friend Alfred Domett returned from New Zealand, the two graying men renewed their old comradship without difficulty. Most gratifying of all these happenings was the discovery that Penini might have a vocation, for the son went to Antwerp to study painting in a good atelier. His first effort there, an oil of "a man looking at a skull," he immediately sent back to his appreciative father.

The father, outwardly warm, outgoing, and comfortable in his afternoon years, was meanwhile contemplating skulls of his own. The four book-length poems on contemporary subjects which proceeded from his pen during the next five years were progressively more clinical and more shocking. *Prince Hohenstiel-Schwangau* (1871) passed as a political oddity, though more than one reviewer thought it dangerous and impudent. But *Fifine at the Fair* (1871) turned out to be a study in the psychology of lechery and adultery; *Red-Cotton Nightcap Country* (early 1873) moved into the psychology of religious madness as expressed in a horrid case of self-mutilation and suicide; and *The Inn Album* (1875) set social degeneracy, adultery, murder, and suicide to competing for the front position. "It grows more difficult every year," Henry James wrote in a review, "for Mr. Browning's old friends to fight his battles for him." Reviewers who had never adopted the category of old friend fired shots like "vicious in conception," "an accumulation of horrors," "bad literary art," "perversion of poetry," "coarse, and even vulgar," "repellant," and "of the clubs, clubby."[2] Not since *Sordello* had Browning laid himself so open to assault, and not one of these four grotesque volumes had a second printing.

II   Prince Hohenstiel-Schwangau: Saviour of Society

Neither Browning nor his wife had developed clear ideas of the historical forces that lie behind politics. In particular, Elizabeth Barrett envisioned political processes as romantic exercises in good and evil, and the dead hand of Elizabeth is easily visible in *Prince Hohenstiel-Schwangau*. Its dubiously unambitious hero is a dwarfed version of her chief hero in contemporary Europe, and its handling of Italian independence and union is an exact postmortem reconstruction of the mechanisms that she had anticipated.

The made-up land of "Hohenstiel-Schwangau" is the fair

land of France; and its deposed Prince, who utters the book as a single monologue, is Louis Napoleon, or Napoleon III. As already suggested, the episodes of Louis Napoleon's policy toward Italy had produced some differences of opinion in the household at Casa Guidi. Elizabeth Barrett, a radical Bonapartist from the beginning, had versified her enthusiasm in one long poem ("Napoleon III in Italy"); and Browning had contemplated, but not written, a poem in answer. The remains of his thought on the subject resided for twelve years in "a little handsbreadth of prose," and were made into the "fullblown bubble" of the book in 1871. By that year the Franco-Prussian War had been stupidly fought and abjectly lost, and Napoleon III was an exile in the undramatic town of Chislehurst, near London. It is in London that the monologue is uttered. The Prince has been flattered into picking up a handsome and uninhibited English lady, and has taken her to a suggestive interior room in a hotel or club. He smokes and talks; she drinks tea and falls asleep. We never quite learn the lady's motives, but the Prince's motive is to explain what his life has been, or, as he carefully distinguishes, what it has seemed to him.

The Prince has not led the type of life that Elizabeth Barrett would have accepted as heroic. He is a more modern specimen, the neutralist who wishes the machinery of the world to run smoothly, but who has no special desire to alter or renovate it. He is the "saviour of society" in the sense that he has rather successfully moderated the lurking extremisms of politics and culture during the twenty years of his rule. In his apprenticeship as a politician, he admits, he has talked much of such absolute concepts as social justice, freedom, and revolution. Having made himself Emperor, however, he finds that his real responsibility lies in keeping the highways open and the people employed:

> Once pedestaled on earth
> To act not speak, I found earth was not air.
> I saw this multitude of mine, and not
> The nakedness and nullity of air
> Fit only for a voice to float in free.
> Such eyes I saw that craved the light alone,
> Such mouths that wanted bread and nothing else,
> Such hands that supplicated handiwork,

> Men with the wives, and women with the babes,
> Yet all these pleading just to live, not die! (902-11)

The Prince identifies with the majority, and prefers not to "risk the whiff of my cigar" for all the ideas of such radical improvers as "Fourier, Compte, and all that ends in air." Let thought love thought, he argues, and men love men:

> Be Kant crowned king of the castle in the air!
> Hans Slouch,—his own, his children's mouths to feed
> In the hovel on the ground,—wants meat, nor chews
> "The Critique of Pure Reason" in exchange.
> .   .   .   .   .   .
> Do not mistake me. You too have your rights!
> Hans must not burn Kant's house above his head
> Because he cannot understand Kant's book:
> And still less must Hans' pastor burn Kant's self
> Because Kant understands some books too well.
> But, justice seen to on this little point,
> Answer me, is it manly, is it sage,
> To stop and struggle with arrangements here
> It took so many lives, so much of toil,
> To tinker up into efficiency? (1108-11, 1146-55)

His "service to humanity," as he understands it, has been careful control of progress—a gentle harmonizing of present and future. He argues that "to have held the balance straight/For twenty years" has been "right usage of my power of head and heart/And reasonable piety besides."

Not all of the Prince's arguments are so consistent and acceptable as these. In the second half especially, the Prince takes to drifting, and lines of argument are confused by such new elements as a tableau staged by the deity "Sagacity" and by repetitious speculations about speculations imputed to political idealists popular at midcentury. Is it in respect to Elizabeth Barrett that Browning makes the Prince utter his single mean inconsistency? The Prince has steadily abjured that tampering with "arrangements" which is done with armies. He is not his grandfather, to smash the world into a "smooth/Uniform mound wherein to plant your flag,/The lily-white, above the blood and brains." He holds that "war for sake/Of the good war gets you as war's sole excuse/Is damnable and damned." But Browning lets him argue, and apparently prove, that French campaigning which supported the unification of Italy was honorable and pious. In the tritest of all war-cries, he calls it "war for the sake of peace." Elizabeth's political heat had led her to be bloodthirsty about this single issue, and Browning lets his Prince set forth the position with a judgmental severity that is in harsh disagreement with his moderate attitudes on every other point.

III   Fifine at the Fair

Placed beside other poems in the difficult categories of society and politics, *Prince Hohenstiel-Schwangau* shines brightly enough; the first half is especially brilliant for its convincingly argued presentation of the case for relaxed government. But *Fifine at the Fair,* a compilation of arguments presenting the case for adultery, has won considerably more attention and interest.

As with the earlier poem, *Fifine at the Fair* is more lively and forward-going in the first half, where there is an actual presence of the adolescent showgirl Fifine, and where Browning's fleshiest and most suggestive writing is employed in bringing Fifine to life. For the speaker of the poem, which again is all one monologue, Browning constructed a unique poetic form embodying twelve-syllable lines rhyming as couplets. These are divided into 132 verse-paragraphs often enjambed by fusion of broken-off lines and couplets. A prologue called "Amphibian" (sometimes anthologized as a separate poem) and an epilogue called "The Householder" express obliquely cautionary views towards the strange, long poem compressed between them.

This poem has only three characters. Don Juan is young, elegant, and "frantic to be free"—freedom for him having a philosophical bearing which goes beyond mere lust. He is married to Elvire, a person spiritual, fleshless, and overrefined, dressed in "as multiplied a coating as protects/An onion from the eye," apparently unable to feel warmth or sympathy for social losers like Fifine, and tending to "draw back skirts from filth like her." Don Juan's feelings towards his wife vary considerably as he speaks to her. At best, he is bored by her virtuous solemnity; at worst, he shows an active dislike for her narrowness, her failure of human sympathy, and the frustrating female weapons system she reserves for use against him. His conversational tone towards her also varies, running from plain mockery to apparently serious argumentation. At the end, he simply lies to her and does not care whether she believes him or not.

In sharpest contrast to Elvire is little naked Fifine, who neither speaks nor is spoken to. Don Juan honors the gypsy girl for her basic, utilitarian, and unpretending view of herself and her relation to a harsh and contemptuous world. To him, she is "though mischievous and mean/Yet free and flowerlike too, with loveliness for law/And self-sustainment made morality." Conceding the squalor and abjectness of her life, he is very stern against that self-approving refinement which would suggest an essential difference between Fifine and women who have had better luck. Don Juan is not sentimental about girls, and he means to sleep with Fifine; but he will not agree to her dehumanization in the thinking of hard, pure women like Elvire.

The long set of insights and arguments which compose the bulk of the poem emphasize human freedom, the suspicious disparity between mankind's religions, the uncertainty of premises underlying ethics, and the two single certainties of sex and death. One long flight of poetry covers a vision or dream Don Juan has had—of a carnival in Venice, of people in masks, of houses, courts, and cathedrals, all steadily losing form and individuation, all steadily blending in the rush towards death. In another flight, which blends with this, Don Juan compares two Druid structures commemorating Death and Sex which were still to be seen at Pornic. One of these ruins is hive-shaped, hollow, and meant to honor some god by demonstrating that "we and earth and all things come and go." An unsatisfactory structure. More satisfactory and cheery, a structure "our grandmothers danced round," is a great stone phallus:

> a huge stone pillar, once upright,
> Now laid at length, half lost—discreetly shunning sight
> In the bush and briar, because of stories in the air—
> Hints what it signified, and why was stationed there,
> Once on a time. (2104-08)

Christ's church, says Don Juan, hates the phallus and has

pulled it down. But, as he tells Elvire, it "bides/Its time to rise again." Moreover, modern scholars "pert from Paris" are explaining that the steeples of Christ's own churches are phallic too—"the symbol's self, expressed in slate for rock." No amount of preaching or scholarizing, says Don Juan, has prevailed against the thesis expressed by the shaft—the thesis, that is, that life, joy, and victory are obtainable only through the flesh as expressed in sex.

Don Juan is made to look sophistical and light in a single verse-paragraph at the end of the poem. Otherwise he seems humane and serious; and his arguments for pleasure, self-expression, and love, all by means of uncodified sex, are at least as successful as the arguments which could be mounted against them. A number of reviewers were unable to decide whether these arguments represented the opinions, or only the perversity, of the writer. Even such a friendly and understanding critic as Alexandra Orr wrote that she was puzzled, and "found it impossible to see where Mr. Browning ends and where Don Juan begins."[3] Browning, who helped Mrs. Orr in some other problems of interpretation, made no attempt to help her in this. He was still in the position of "dramatic" writer, and consequently able to assert that the positions taken in poems were the positions of the people in the poems.

IV Red-Cotton Nightcap Country

In *Red-Cotton Nightcap Country* (subtitled *Turf and Towers*) blossoms a true story of the confusion and eventual suicide of the heir to an international jewelry firm. Abandoning the monologue form for the first time since *Sordello*, Browning tells the story in the third person, his primary auditor being his old friend Anne Thackeray, and the reader being allowed, as it were, to overhear what is said. A debt is acknowledged at the beginning. Miss Thackeray, as we are told at great length, has found the pointed caps of the Norman peasantry amusing and has proposed to write a book about the region under the title "White-Cotton Nightcap Country." Browning now suggests the better appropriateness of "Red-Cotton" by virtue of a lurid event of a few months back and of the sensational court trial which has just been completed. The question of whether the lady will agree to the propriety of "Red-Cotton" when the story of the dead heir is complete provides a specious but good-humored element of challenge.

The story itself is strong enough. An international jewel firm, the Mirandas (in real life, the Mellorios) have produced an heir, Leónce, whose passions are divided between worldly pleasure and religious aspiration. The code for the first is "turf," and for the second, "towers." After some wenching in Paris, Leónce falls in love with Clara, a married woman with a spotted past but pure intentions. Mutual devotion makes them man and wife in all but name. They retreat to the former priory of Clairvaux, which Leónce's father has been using as a summer home, and there build an English park and an enormous stucco fairy-palace surmounted by a towering lookout post—the worldly pleasures of turf and the heavenly ones of towers combining in the single edifice. A crisis comes with the death of Leónce's mother under circumstances which make Leónce hold himself responsible.

This new guilt is too much to bear. Temporarily separated from the more realistic Clara, Leónce responds by burning his two guilty hands off at the wrist. Reunited to Clara, returned to Clairvaux, still craving the best of this life and also the next, he leads a sybaritic life of hunting, riding, loving, and painting; but he simultaneously focuses his religious attentions, and his purse, on the Church. On a final day, cheerfully intending a ride, and waiting for his horse to be saddled, Leónce idly climbs to the upper deck of his tower. Miles away, the steepled Virgin of Ravissante seems to be beckoning him. He has always believed in miracles, and it strikes him that the miracle of being carried to the Lady by her own angels would successfully resolve the dilemmas of his life. Churchmen have refused to marry him to Clara; but if the Virgin approves of him, and has her angels carry him safely from his tower to her distant steeple, the mark of her favor will extend to the liaison, and sanctify it as a marriage. Secure in his faith, he takes his "sublime spring" from "the tower so often talked about" and moves to a position "stone-dead . . . on the turf."

In view of his earlier behavior, we tend to think Leónce's last deed a neurotic or psychotic one. The failed injunction "thou shalt not tempt the lord thy God" has particular cogency because it was uttered by the Christ under a similar temptation on a similar high place. But Browning finds Leónce's deed perfectly sane, given the premises; and he takes pride in showing that, in the actual Mellorio instance, both church and state had made a similar finding. He draws a number of other morals as the tale proceeds, but the main moral, the thesis of the whole, is that a man had better make a choice of goals and support his choice with vigor, rather than drifting between opposing goals as did Leónce. We need not approve of the intrusion of such morals in what is mainly a study of morbid psychology, nor of the seemingly endless ornamentation via the colloquy with Miss Thackeray, nor of the generally ugly attitude Browning takes towards the Catholic Church and its clergymen. When DeVane in his *Handbook* twice calls the main story "sordid," he apparently refers to the long cohabitation of Leónce and Clara, a curious turn, since that is the single element which Browning presents as pure, loving, and generous from beginning to end.

V   The Inn Album

A comment placed by William Dean Howells in the *Atlantic Monthly* may be added to the critical comments cited at the beginning of the chapter. *The Inn Album*, Howells said, was a "curiously wilful piece of bad literary art which its attempts to outlaw itself cannot render in any degree interesting, save for the first moment of surprise."[4] The concept of self-outlawry adduced by Howells has some critical utility. The main influences bearing on *The Inn Album* were a modernist crime-album play by Fanny Kemble, the reportage of the celebrated law case of "The Tichbourne Claimant," the analytic Realism of Balzac, and (the source mainly alleged by Browning) a men's club story about a notorious gambler and rake, the Lord De Ros. That Browning's literary objectives were immediacy, originality, and moral shock is obvious throughout. The form he chose, apparently for its swifter movement, was drama for four voices.

Predictability is the hallmark of *The Inn Album*. We may name its people, since Browning did not. Let us call them Sir Rudolph Rasmussen, Hunter Armstrong, Magdalen Overlove, and Pansy Greenacres. Rasmussen, brother to a duke, is a worldly clubman and gambler, but too old and too poor to support his role. Armstrong, a beautiful, broad-necked young clubman, has sought to learn the ways of the world at the feet of Rasmussen. Magdalen, though still in her midtwenties, has experienced both the pure love of Armstrong, then an Oxford student, and a cold-blooded seduction by the experienced Rasmussen. Neither man knows, at first, the part he has played in her now-ruined life. Pansy Greenacres, Armstrong's cousin and bride-elect, is a cheerful, pretty, high-spirited heiress of twenty. The scene is the parlor of a country inn, with some divagation in the surrounding fields; and the action is compressed into five or six hours.

All these conditions make for comedy and would have been appropriate for the plays of Etheredge or Sheridan. Browning attempts tragedy and achieves melodrama. As the play opens, Rasmussen and Armstrong are finishing a night of cards; and, instead of winning as expected, Rasmussen has lost some ten thousand unpayable pounds. Armstrong's purpose in the visit is to pay court to his cousin Pansy in her manor nearby. Pansy has meanwhile summoned her older friend Magdalen to advise her about the marriage. When Rasmussen and Magdalen encounter each other in the inn parlor, they immediately launch fierce and lengthy attacks on one another. Armstrong returns, finds that Magdalen is the girl he has loved among the dreaming spires of Oxford, and must cope with the double shock of learning that she has "fallen" and that she has arranged to do a lifetime of penance by marrying a stupid old clergyman and living in a squalid backwoods parish. After some attitude-taking by Armstrong and Magdalen, the practical Rasmussen develops a plan. Under threat of telling her clergyman-husband about her past, he will force Magdalen to become the mistress of Armstrong, who may meanwhile continue with his plans to marry the heiress Pansy. Rasmussen's stipend for arranging the immoral liaison will be cancellation of his ten thousand pound indebtedness. The only possible loser in this arrangement would be Magdalen, whose new and permanent status would be that of an open courtesan. After hearing the neat plan, young Armstrong leaps across the room and kills Rasmussen with a single blow. The view of herself as a gambling trophy defeats Magdalen, who takes poison. With cheerfully inconsequent discourse, wholly unsuspecting, the innocent Pansy arrives at the parlor door, and opens it—"No: let the curtain fall," cries the author, and the tale is over.

It would be wrong to call *The Inn Album* uninteresting. Utter contemporaneousness is achieved: here are railroads, men's clubs, Monte Carlo, London cliques, Disraeli, Gladstone, Tennyson, Carlyle, Ruskin, and Anthony Trollope, whose novels Pansy speaks of reading "as penance." Browning cheerfully introduces the stalest of current views about himself:

> Yon bard's a Browning, he neglects the form;
> But oh the sense, ye Gods, the weighty sense!

Some nice ironies come from inappropriate entries made in the inn album by former travelers. But the values of the play, and to a large extent its relationships, would be vulgar and conventional in any aspect save that of comedy. Wronged or "pure," the three young people are stereotypes. The single three-dimensional character, Rasmussen, interests us at the beginning by his coolness, modesty, and unpretending attitude towards things as they are, but gradually loses his attractiveness as his villainies become darker and more self-oriented. Eventually, he is reduced to the stock villain-character whom writers of melodrama may produce by the dozen.

VI *Summary of the Down Beat*

The Inn Album, the last of the four naturalistic books which had begun with *Prince Hohenstiel-Schwangau,* was to most readers the least acceptable. The poet who had won national acclaim with *The Ring and the Book* was now as vulnerable to moral disdain as either Swinburne or William Morris. The turn had been radical, it was now about to be reversed, and some general reflections about the books seem in order.

First, a simple homogeneity exists in the four books. However unlike in cast and form, each of them emphasizes socially unacceptable acts and attitudes; and each lacks anything that might be called heroism, or even a hero. Second, they body forth a steady incrementation of squalor and violence of motivation. Browning increasingly lets himself be known as an "analyst," and in that role analyzes abstract truth and goodness almost out of existence. Accompanying this diminution of mankind is a diminution of cheer in the surroundings. Each milieu seems less attractive than the one before. Third, we need to remember that these four books fell from the press interspersed with the three Greek books of Browning. We might argue therefore that the modern quartet absorbed the darker and uglier thrusts of Browning's intellect, while the Hellenic trio absorbed the sunnier and higher. An equally possible suggestion would envision the Greek and the modern books as proceeding on the same downward course, especially in regard to the common literary culture of Browning's own time. There needs to be a study of Browning's total output from 1871 to 1877, and it should have the object of either separating the two groups or drawing them more closely together.

And what of techniques? In the fourth place, we see in the structure of both groups a serious attempt of Browning to escape the monologue form and perhaps the casuistical motive as well. In the period about to begin, Browning's tendency will be to speak in his own voice, and to utter views, exculpations, and judgments not as an isolated character might see them but as he himself does. Fifth and finally, we find each of the four books written in a clearer and more forthright style than the one before. By the time of *The Inn Album*, it was possible for some critics to charge Browning with plain prose-writing, and one or two did. But he had obviously grown weary of hearing his verse decried as tangled, knotted, and uncouth, and was obviously seeking a nearer approach to the plainness and lucidity for which Arnold and Tennyson were being praised. Unfortunately, he had been typecast, and his shifts were little noticed by critics. The righteous fury which exploded in his next book, *Pacchiarrotto*, is at least partly to be attributed to the blindness of journals and journalists to reforms which they themselves had enjoined.

CHAPTER 11

Five Volumes on Forty Themes

I *The World of a Number of Things*

UPON completion of his three Greek volumes and his four modern ones, Browning turned away from book-length poems. The canon after about 1875 is a great emporium of themes, forms, styles, and manners. Browning's life at this time was not only comfortable but highly enjoyable. He had become one of the major personages of Britain and America; his income was in good condition; his son Penini worked seriously at painting; his health was excellent, and the energy and desire to write poetry continued to rise within him. Vigorous, confident, and self-assured, he was what the Spanish call a "green old man," and his work was now for himself: he did what he liked.

Of the five volumes now to be glanced at, *Pacchiarotto and How He Worked in Distemper* (1876) is the longest and the most mixed in content. An interesting paradox lies in the fact that, while much of the volume attacks those who would look into poets' personal lives and thoughts, it offers the most naked and unguarded set of subjective statements in the whole body of Browning's work. The one-volume collection of *La Saisiaz, The Two Poets of Croisic*, and some outriding prologues and epilogues (1878) addressed itself directly to nineteenth-century intellectual problems which Browning still hoped to help settle. *Dramatic Idylls,* [First Series] (1879), and *Dramatic Idylls*, Second Series (1880), return to Browning's cautionary use of "Dramatic" in volumes of decades earlier and to the original signification of Idyll as a simple narrative of (usually) simple and rough life told in suitably simple and rough language.

Browning's title for the volume *Jocoseria* (1883) was borrowed from a collection of believe-it-or-not stories collected by Otto Melander and published in 1597. Describing the contents of this last of his random volumes, Browning used the expression "a collection of things gray*ish* and gay*ish*." Hardly six weeks after publication, he wrote to a friend: "this little *Jocoseria* (joking even in the title), has had the usual luck of the little deserving,—got itself sold . . . at the rate of 2000 copies very early, and is now reprinting."[1] The fact that an almost unheard-of third edition quickly followed the second attests to the intense interest which Browning by then commanded.

II   Pacchiarotto: *of Art and Criticism*

The prologue, the epilogue, the title piece, and five other poems in the *Pacchiarotto* volume refer directly to the relationships which may subsist between the makers of art and the users of it. Like most of Browning's prologues, this one refers to Elizabeth Barrett. It is suggested that she is waiting behind "an old wall" and that a reunion may be effected. However, the poet adds some blows at the lack of personal privacy which has been a hateful result of his fame, and speaks of his own "ruddy strife" and lips "whence storm-clouds start" as obvious references to the reprisal the book is about to make.

It was severe reprisal. "At the Mermaid," "House," and "Shop" are all devoted to the defense of privacy and to abuses imputed by literary journalists, in particular Alfred Austin. "At the Mermaid" is a monologue uttered in lively eight-lined stanzas supposedly spoken by Shakespeare to Ben Jonson. It refers directly to Austin's several-times-printed belief that neither Tennyson nor Browning was capable of first-rate work, and that Britain still awaited its next master-poet. Ben Jonson's suggestion that Shakespeare might be a suitable "next poet" (following Spenser) is rejected with humorous scorn by the man of Stratford. As "next poet," would he not have to endure journalistic indignities? In Browning's view, Shakespeare had deliberately sought to keep his life obscure and his "rarities" unknown. Some references to the departed "last poet" point to both Wordsworth and Byron, and there is a continuing insistence that the "next" master poet might be forced into the roles of hermit, man-hater, malcontent, or suicide.

In the simpler poem, "House," Browning declares that his private life belongs within a domestic structure, hidden by thick walls from the smirch of "men's eyes." Here occur the

well-known demurrer from Wordsworth's view (in "Scorn not
the Sonnet") that Shakespeare had "unlocked his heart" in
his Sonnets. Browning responded, "Did Shakespeare? If so,
the less Shakespeare he." Much of the companion poem,
"Shop," is a description of a store that is full of interesting
items, all open to the view and to the handling of any passer-by.
The owner this time has no house, but lies at the "back of
all that spread/Of merchandise." He is, to open the metaphor,
ready to display his own every act, emotion, and belief to
anyone interested in his wares. Browning's argument twists
somewhat at the end of the poem, where instead of mere
residential privacy ("a Mayfair" or "Hampstead villa") he asks
that each man have more than one main interest, or residence.
Our hearts, he concludes, should be "Christ, how far!" from
the "sorts of treasure" displayed in our stores.

"Pacchiarotto, and How He Worked in Distemper" runs
counter to the adjurations of "House" and "Shop" by display-
ing all the personal rancor Browning had developed toward
Alfred Austin and the whole critical profession. The poem
is written in aggressive, cacaphonic, usually octosyllabic couplets, with wild double and triple rhymes such as "out-
side/louts eyed," and, in ferocious reference to Austin's
dwarfish figure, inadequate verse, and love of Byron, "Quilp
Hop-o-my-thumb there/Banjo Byron that twangs the strum-
strum there." The name Pacchiarotto had originally belonged
to a Siennese painter who, as Austin seemed to do, belonged
to a coterie of men who found fault with everything but produced remedies for nothing. One day, says Browning, his sting-
ing having become excessive, Pacchiarotto was attacked,
humiliated, and forced to hide in a grave with a rotting corpse.
Emerging after some days, a stinking ruin of a man, he proposes
to be more careful but is essentially unreformed.

Browning takes leave of the bygone Siennese to introduce
a supposed modern army of critics and critical journals who
invade his premises in the form of chimney sweeps who "bring
more filth into my house/Than ever you found there." Some
hundred lines of rather pure vituperation follow. Austin, like
others, had charged Browning with careless grammar and
obscurity "of words that convey thought." Austin's own words,
replied the poet, conveyed "ignorance, impudence, envy,/And
malice" with a "clearness crystalline." Austin, who became

"next poet" in a way by succeeding Tennyson in the Laureate-
ship, went on deploring the inadequacy of Victorian poetry.
As a girl, Maisie Ward knew Austin very well, and she remem-
bered how the little old man parodied Browning's dedication
of *The Ring and the Book*, beginning "Oh lyric love, half angel
and half bird," as "his lyric love, half governess, half bore."[2]
Browning was dead and presumably did not hear.

Two other poems related to the arts are "Cenciaja" and
"Filippo Baldinucci on the Privilege of Burial." The murder
which had given rise to Shelley's play *The Cenci* had been
mentioned in legal documents bearing on the murder of Pompilia Franceschini, and Browning versified the material to
illustrate Shelley's "superb/Achievement by a rescued anecdote." The three hundred lines of blank verse which follow
narrate the brutal murder of the Marchesa dell' Oriolo by her
sons, an act which had toughened the Pope's thinking about
murders within families and encouraged him to order the
execution of Shelley's heroine Beatrice Cenci. More sparkle
and interest appear in "Fillipo Baldinucci." In galloping eight-
lined stanzas, Browning permits the prolific art-historian Baldinucci (fl. 1700) to tell a century-old tale about a trick and
countertrick involving a couple of mean Christians and the
Jewish community of Florence. As a direct insult, a farmer
whose land overlooked the Jewish cemetery outside Florence
built a chapel and had Buti (fl. 1600), a hack artist, ornament
the side facing the graves with a huge mural of the Virgin.
The Jews arranged, for a large sum, to have the insulting Virgin
moved to another wall of the chapel. After taking the money,
the farmer and Buti did move Mary around the building, but
they replaced her with a still more insulting mural of Christ
crucified. The cheated congregation is naturally furious. Its
revenge comes rather subtly, however, when a rich, tough
young Jew ("a six-feet-high herculean-build/Young he-Jew
with a beard that baulks/Description") enters Buti's studio,
scares Buti and the farmer out of their wits, and then mildly
buys some of Buti's religious painting. He will place it in
his collection with the Venuses and Tritons and other dead
gods, he says, and so reduce the Virgin, Saviour, or whatever,
to mere unmeaning secular technique. The poem is full of
vivid and humorous detail, and the half-worried, half-scared
tones of the speaker Baldinucci are most amusing.

In the "Epilogue," Browning returns to direct attack. Using as his major metaphor wine-tasting, Browning finds that pretentiously superfine drinkers, which is to say critics, find every vintage too sweet or too dry, too new or too old—always too something. He moves around the vintages of some poets before him, and tries out some other metaphors of less emphasis. But he concludes with drink again. Why wine at all? Poisonous nettles will "make a broth/Wholesome for blood grown lazy and thick." His "friends who are sound" may still quaff magnums of the best. But he will physic bad readers "nothing loth/Henceforward with nettle-broth." Critics might take warning from that.

III Pacchiarotto: *What You Will*

Hardly offsetting the mood of anger which distinguishes the anti-critic poems of *Pacchiarotto* is the mood of dubiety and frustration which distinguish the miscellaneous poems. Since 1920 or so it has been customary to blame the negativism of these poems chiefly on the emotional outcome of Browning's courtship of Lady Ashburton. The courtship itself had failed; and, as the argument goes, Browning had to face the far deeper failure of his often-vowed fidelity to his dead wife. It seems more reasonable to think that both anger and sadness resulted from the knowledge that, through a typical overreaction, he had imprisoned his vigorous and adventurous ego in the pale role of "eternal lover." The evidence of *Pacchiarotto* and several other volumes supports the latter view.

Some of the poems in *Pacchiarotto* are exempt. "Hervé Reil" and "A Forgiveness," two long narrative poems, hark back to years before Browning's widowhood or before his marriage. The historical piece "Hervé Riel" cheerfully recounts how the seamanship and courage of a simple sailor save an entire French fleet from destruction by the English; and the sailor's modest evaluation of the great feat gives the poem its slight psychological punch. "A Forgiveness" is pure fiction, and compares with such earlier horror-poems as "The Laboratory" and "The Confessional." In the plot, one melodramatic enough, a dedicated, hard-working statesman of the court of Spain finds that his young wife has taken a priest for her lover. Rather than seeking revenge at once, he works on for three years, treating the lady in all ways as before. At last, broken down

from nervous anxiety, the lady insists on explaining the motives
behind her sin. She always loved her husband, she says, but
had become jealous of his career:

> Double dyed
> In folly and guilt, I thought you gave
> Your heart and soul away from me to slave
> At statecraft. Since my right in you seemed lost
> I stung myself to teach you, to your cost,
> What you rejected could be prized beyond
> Life, heaven, by the first fool I threw a fond
> Look on, a fatal word to.

Accepting the paradox that she has done adultery to hurt herself, to hurt him, to teach him, and all for love, the grandee
elegantly forgives both parties. The two ensuing murders are
also elegant—he cuts the lady's breast a little so that she may
write her confession in blood, as she desires, but does the
cutting with a dagger not only jeweled but poisoned. And
he confesses the whole affair to his priest, who is also his
wife's priest, before sabering him through the grating of the
confessional booth.

Two shorter poems that are also exempt from the presiding
malaise of the volume are "Natural Magic" and "Magical
Nature." The second of these love lyrics is a mechanical conceit: the beloved one is no flower but a jewel, for in durability
a jewel is "at no mercy of a moment." In the better developed
"Natural Magic," the speaker is found thrusting a naked
nautch-girl into a room "quite as bare." Upon his reopening
the door, he discovers the room "not bare, but embowered
/With—who knows what verdure, O'erfruited, o'erflowered?"
His heart, as he explains in the second part, was equally barren;
and barren was the lady he admitted into it. In both cases
Love has been the magician who invoked the foliage, flowers,
and fruits, where none should have grown at all.

In "Pisgah-Sights I" and "Pisgah-Sights II," the two poems
which lead off the miscellany section of *Pacchiarotto*, Browning assumes the role of a dying man who is able to see over
great tracts of experience, just as the dying Moses did when
looking down from Mount Pisgah. But Browning looks back
in despair, while Moses had looked forward in joy. In his

first "sight," Browning (or his speaker) observes "one recon-
cilement" in all the apparent opposites and contraries of the
world. His regret is having been picky and judgmental, and
not accepting it all. Now, "There's life lying/And I see all
of it,/Only, I'm dying." In "Pisgah-Sights II," he still more
emphatically praises acquiescence and acceptance. He should
not have aspired; he should have been "earth's native"; he
must not be "creative/Chopping and changing it." The poem
"Fears and Scruples" returns to Western myths, or at least
to doubts about them. "Of old" the speaker has loved an
"unseen friend" known to him only by "letters." But the friend,
Christ, now keeps silent and absent, leaving the field to scorn-
ers and disbelievers. At the end is offered the appalling possibility that the friend is a "monster" who, never having made
himself visible, will now deal out punishments to persons
who have not seen him.

"St. Martin's Summer," "Bifurcation," and "Appearances"
deal with unsatisfactory love relationships. "St. Martin's Summer" ("Indian Summer" to Americans) imagines in eighteen
six-line stanzas the gradual intervention of "ghosts" between
two people who suppose themselves in love. Browningite
dogma has always regarded the former spouses of Browning
and Lady Ashburton as the ghosts in question, but it is not
necessary to add the biographical context since the poem
makes equally good sense as portraying the growing conviction
of the speaker that the "young princess" whom he wishes
to love is no integral human but a concatenation of images
which his own wishes have brought together. Read in this
way, the poem would as easily refer to the poet's construct
of Elizabeth Barrett, who might not be the real Elizabeth Barrett, as to the Baroness or any other woman.

"Bifurcation" ("forking off" in Greek) gives in compact blank
verse the supposed epitaphs of a woman and man, "two lovers,"
who have elected different routes. The woman has eschewed
fleshly consummation because of a conflicting "duty," but the
man has chosen total love at whatever cost. It has been the
woman's facile view that "heaven repairs what wrong earth's
journey did," and she suggests consummation in Heaven. The
man, outliving her, has begun to think that her easy common-
places may have disguised weakness, selfishness, and hypocrisy. Rather angrily, he asks that their two decisions be

inscribed on their two tombs after which some wise man may "acquaint/The simple—which holds sinner, which holds saint." The twelve clear lines of "Appearances" are an undisguished statement about betrayal of a man by a woman. In a "poor room" the woman pledges a troth which is hinted to have an unusual clau.e or so. In a "rich room," a little later, "The other word was spoken; ask/This rich room how you dropped the mask!" When, why, how? If a real woman was meant, it was not Lady Ashburton, who plighted no troth and wore no mask.

Besides the anger expressed in all of them, what joins these three poems together is their uniform presentation of women as the tormenters of men by the agency of deception and disguise. From the male point of view, the most untrue yet most tormenting woman in *Pacchiarotto* is the female of "Numpholeptos." The Greek title of this strange poem translates into "slave of a nymph"; and its nymph is a hybrid of woman and goddess whose destiny it is to attract passion but not to reciprocate it. The nymph of the poem is a creature of "central light." White light runs out from this center in rays, and the speaker is dispatched along these, his mission always being to have a full experience of the world prismed impurely to colors, but to return to its center still as spotless, pure, and white as the center itself. The world being what it is, however, the man must inevitably return battered, soiled, and smeared with "crocus, saffron, orange . . . /Scarlet, purple, every dye of the bow." Having no potential for empathy, the nymph can recognize neither her cruelty nor the man's frustration. At best, returning so smeared, the man gets "a sad, slow, silver smile," and at worst he gets "looks harsh and hard—/Forbearance, then repulsion, then disdain." Towards his agonies her soul is "blank." At one point, trying to rebel, he speaks of her in familiar male-female judgments:

> O you—less hard
> And hateful than mistaken and obtuse
> Unreason of a she-intelligence!
> You very woman with the pert pretense
> To match the male achievement!
>   . . . O that ear
> All fact pricks rudely, that thrice-superfine

> Femininity of sense, with right divine
> To waive all process, take result stain-free
> From out the very muck wherein—

The speaker, who himself breaks off these accusations, recognizes them as merely "the true slave's querulous outbreak." The psychological naturalism of the lines suggests, in this case at least, a biographical connection. This suggestion is reinforced by Browning's connection of his white nymph to "that pale soft sweet disempassioned moon/That smiles me slow forgiveness." The moon was Browning's persistent symbol for Elizabeth Barrett. If the nymph had an earthly model, we can guess her name.

Betty Miller's pages explicating this poem are worth reading, as is her general account of the "strange deterioration" which took place "posthumously, as it were, in the relationship of husband and wife."[3] As has been hinted in this study, the deteriorating relationship may have included the Ashburton fiasco as a symptom of Browning's self-blame rather than as the cause of it. Julia Wedgwood, his most intimate friend in 1868, the year before the Ashburton year, did not particularly like *The Ring and the Book*, and was so bold as to suggest that he may have spent "all these years on a mistake." Browning's defiant answer was, "I have given four full years to this 'mistake,' but what did I do with my fourteen years in Italy?"[4] Miss Wedgwood could hardly have interpreted the question. "Numpholeptos" was still to be written, but in it Browning gives a reasonably acceptable interpretation.

IV *Immortalities:* La Saisiaz *and* the Two Poets

In a single volume, in 1878, Browning published *La Saisiaz* and *The Two Poets of Croisic*, a short prologue for each, and a hundred-line epilogue intended to wrap up the whole book. Except that they once more bid hello to Elizabeth Barrett, neither prologue is of much interest. The epilogue borrows from a poem in the Greek Anthology the pretty story of a minstrel who breaks a lyre-string while competing for a prize, but is saved by a cricket which providentially lights on the instrument and utters exactly the missing note. In the "application" which follows, the saving sound of the cricket is linked to the saving sound of a girl's voice saying "Love."

La Saisiaz and *The Two Poets* deal philosophically and then comically with lives after death, a subject still newsworthy in 1878. *La Saisiaz* represents the serious, and apparently honest, thinking of Browning himself on the subject of the immortality of the soul. The scene is the sloping country near Geneva; and the inspiring personage is Ann Egerton Smith, a very old and trusted friend, Browning's confidante since the days of the Fox and Flower circles of his early manhood. Miss Smith had died suddenly in the villa of La Saisiaz where she was summering with Browning and his sister. Just previous to her death, the three aging Britons had been discussing a running debate on immortality in the journal *Nineteenth Century*. Browning, suddenly heartsick, and still full of thought, gave his views in the "Locksley Hall Stanza" which Tennyson had domesticated for use in poems of faith and doubt. Lurking in the intellectual wings are Voltaire, Rousseau, Gibbon, Byron, and Shelley, all of whom had lived in the region before Browning, and all of whose scoffing souls seemed poised to pounce on Browning's effort.

Browning's effort is not on the whole laughable. Making up parts of the argument are the relative weakness of human reason as opposed to imagination, and of evidence as opposed to desire. The paradox most appealed to is the pain and torment of life in conjunction with the concept of "meaning." His model of the sentient world in general was that "Nature red in fang and claw" which so appalled the Victorian sense of fairness:

Every clime I turn my eyes from, as in one or other stage
Of a torture writhe they, Job-like, couched on dung and crazed
      with blains—
Wherefore? Whereto? ask the whirlwind what the dread voice
      thence explains!
I shall "vindicate no way of God's to man," nor stand apart,
"Laugh, be candid!" while I watch it traversing the human heart.
Traversed heart must tell its story uncommented on.

His own beliefs are free, Browning says. They arise from his own decision, and he does not try to sell them. His own life, in which "Sorrow did and joy did nowise,—life well weighed,—preponderate," would need to be regarded as futile unless applied to an eschatological context, but he does not insist on an objective or universal application. Finally, he simply renounces argument; All the good arguments are on the side of Voltaire, Gibbon, Byron. The last and sufficient excuse for faith arises from that splendid Victorian concept of public responsibility. The mass of men, he says, are not so powerful as Byron, so learned as Gibbon, so witty as Voltaire. The mass of men, in their suffering lives, must take "flame for evidence" and "find significance in fireworks." Browning refuses to mock their beliefs, as do other eminent men. In simple generosity, he suggests, he has turned his mind over to these needy, hurt humans, and will let them say of him:

> He there, with the brand flamboyant, broad o'er night's forlorn abyss,
> Crowned by prose and verse; and wielding, with Wit's bauble,
>   Learning's rod—
> Well? Why, he at least believed in Soul, was very sure of God.

Public responsibility can hardly be carried farther than this.

The Two Poets of Croisic is a narrative poem written in very sprightly eight-lined stanzas. Its lighter concern is immortality through poetry, or actually the casual accidentality of literary history, for both René Gentilhomme (born 1610) and Paul Desforges-Maillard (born about 1710) survive because of biographical anecdote rather than the merit of their work. René was a poet-page in the court of that Duke of Condé who was cousin to the childless King Francis and believed certain to become King thereafter. In Browning's story, he witnesses the falling-down of the Duke's sculptured crest; wildly prophesies that the King will have a son, thus blasting the Duke's chances; and sets the prophesy down in the bad verses ("rubbish unutterable") which represented his best talent. Meanwhile, the King is actually welcoming a son into the world. René, suddenly revealed as prophet as well as poet, is called to the royal court to be the King's own laureate. His work is printed, his portrait painted, his pension worked out. Once established as a national figure, however, he neither writes nor prophesies:

> All this burst of fame
> Fury of favor, Royal Poetship,
> Prophetship, book, verse, picture—thereof came—Nothing!

A century later, his fellow citizen Paul could not even find a copy of his "Works," a mere "fifty leaves in duodecime."

Paul's story, like René's, is about quick fame followed by nothing. After some regional success as a writer of *vers de société*, the "dapper gentleman" Paul seeks greater themes and national fame. He is rebuffed in turn by the French Academy and by the celebrated journal *Mercure*. At his sister's suggestion, he resubmits his work under a woman's name. Now it finds enthusiastic acceptance; and not only La Roque, the editor of the *Mercure*, but that "sharpest, shrewdest steel that ever stabbed/To death Imposture," the analytic genius Voltaire, extols the work and falls in love with the supposed poetess. The hoax ends as hoaxes do; and, operating under his own name again, Paul sinks back into obscurity and silence.

These charming stories are charmingly told. From them, as Sir Frederick Kenyon remarked, "Browning, according to his custom,... deduces somewhat unexpected morals."[5] René's silence after his experience of revelation and prophecy is justified, for no one can go higher than such an experience, and there is no point in working below one's peak. Paul's success or failure is to be judged by his acceptance of the event. The "simple test" by which one may judge "the worth of poets" is inquiry as to "which one led a happy life." In urging that reputation counts for nothing Browning strikes a fresh blow at critics:

> ... Who does not know how the La Roques,
> Voltaires, can say and unsay, praise and blame,
> Prove black white, white black, play at paradox,
> And, when they seem to lose it, win the game.

"Fame," he concludes, is only the "quack, quack, quack" of these and lesser geese.

V   *Two Volumes of* Idyls

The two volumes of *Dramatic Idyls* (1879 and 1880) together contained some twelve poems, most of which are sufficiently anecdotal and story-oriented to make the term "dramatic" improper. Most reviewers generously praised their vigor, their "moral earnestness," and their comparative freedom from contorted grammar. But the single critic who suggested that an unknown author could not have gotten publishers to accept "this sort of thing"[6] was undoubtedly right.

Of the six Idyls in the "First Series," four draw their emotional burden from misdoing, guilt, and punishment. The exceptions are "Pheidippides" and "Tray." In "Pheidippides" Browning uses an unusual sixteen-syllable line to tell of the three major happenings in the life of an Athenian runner—his mission to Sparta, his encounter with the god Pan, and the dash to report victory over the Persians which gave a name to the Marathon Run but was, in that first instance, fatal to the runner. The poem "Tray" is an antivivisectionist poem, one of dozens produced during the second half of the century, and not up to the moderate standard of the volume. Perhaps the most likeable poem of the volume is "Ivan Ivanovich," in which the fullest possible range of human emotion and motivation is displayed.

In a prior action of "Ivan Ivanovich," off stage, an unfortunate woman has enacted one of the most famous deeds in Russian folklore. Driving with her three children over a forest road in midwinter, she finds her sleigh being overtaken by a pack of wolves. One child, then another, and at last her youngest and dearest, are squeezed overside; and each disaster slows the wolf-tribe a little. There has previously been some discourse on the expertise with which Russian workmen use the axe in the place of whole British toolchests—as "a hammer and saw and plane/And chisel, and—what know I else?" With his fellow villagers, the sober and respectable carpenter Ivan Ivanovich listens to the broken-hearted sole survivor tell her story and beg for understanding—and then expertly severs her head with a stroke of his axe. Priests, magistrates, and nobles, as well as villagers, are left to entangle themselves in the law and ethics of the event; but Browning skillfully keeps the reader's attention on the wholly unruffled attitude of Ivan Ivanovich during every step of his act and its aftermath.

"Martin Relph," "Halbert and Hob," and "Ned Bratts" are close to being antipoems. One reviewer called the Bratts poem "a transcendently horrible English nightmare," and the judgment would also fit the others. Degenerate peasantry inhabit them all. During an incident of the Jacobite rebellion of 1745, Martin Relph has failed to save the woman he loves from a firing squad, his reason being that she loves another man. Browning's account of the frantic attempt of the genuine lover to carry a pardon through bureaucracies and military lines is perhaps the most exciting part of this poem. Relph speaks from the madness which is the result of his guilt. The two characters of "Halbert and Hob" are a father and son "Harsh and fierce of word, rough and savage of deed,/Hated and feared." On a Christmas Eve they quarrel viciously with one another. Hob manages to thrust his father out into the storm, but relents when Halbert says, "strangely submissive," that as a youth and on a Christmas he has thrust his own father out in the same way. They return to their chairs in the house. Halbert dies during the night, however, and the son's behavior suddenly turns gentle and submissive, but also insane.

"Ned Bratts" is more moral, though just as ugly. The plot itself is based on one told by John Bunyan in his *Life and Death of Mr. Badman,* the protagonist there being named "old Tod." Like old Tod, Browning's country criminals Ned and Tab break into court, confess their series of crimes, and demand that the judges "make but haste to hang us both." There is the expectable consternation in the court, but "My Lord Chief Justice" sees the matter as capable of double utility. "Forms were galloped through," and Bratts and Tab are "happily hanged forthwith." Meanwhile, sentences laid on other felons by the Court are lessened or waived; and Bunyan himself, a man long jailed, is praised and given a hint of pardon some time in the future.

An anonymous reviewer commented that the *Dramatic Lyrics, Second Series,* happily lacked poems "founded upon the psychology of crime and bloodshed . . . the morbid fondness for which" had so long been "brought as a reproach" against the poet.[7] The critic might have added that, like most sequels, the Second Series lacked much of the zest and force belonging to the First. Once more there are six poems; but only a couple rise above the level of anecdote, and only one, "Pan and Luna," achieves high interest as poetry.

"Echlectos," "Muleykeh," "Pietro of Albano," and "Doctor—" bring their stories from Greek, Arabian, Italian, and Hebrew legendry. "Echlectos" is a salute to an obscure Greek who fought at Marathon, using his plough as a weapon. Honors were voted to him by the state, and a search was made for him, but neither the man nor his name was discovered. The great Oracle advised the troubled Awards Committee to sing hymns to Echlectos, in translation "the plough-bearer," adding that names meant little. "The great deed ne'er grows small,/Not the great name." "Muleykah" takes its name from a "peerless mare," the single glory of an otherwise poor tribesman named Hosein. When his treasure is ridden off by an unskilled thief, Hosein follows and overtakes, though on an inferior horse, and gallantly protects Muleykah from the imputation of slowness by giving the technical advice which allows horse and horsethief to disappear over the pass.

"Pietro of Albano," a cheerfully wicked poem undervalued as a "doggerel lilt" by Sir Frederick Kenyon, tells of a medieval professor of medicine, thought also to be a magician, who by means of hypnotism tricks an upstart student into a false belief in his future glory and success and then into a valid knowledge of his own moral and mental incapacity. "Doctor—" begins "A Rabbi told me" and lightly retells a Talmudic yarn about the contretemps which follow upon Satan's son's taking up the profession of medicine but refusing to take up holy wedlock. Unlike most men, the doctor knows that "Death is the strongest-born of Hell, and yet/Stronger than Death is a Bad Wife." Like the others, "Doctor—" is an amusing bauble based on a quirk of mind and legend, and is perfectly sound as comedy but essentially lightweight.

"Clive" and "Pan and Luna" hold the attention better. "Clive," another of Browning's men's-club stories, retells an incident of the early life of the man whose sagacity and talent culminated in the British domination of India. A lowly clerk in a dull garrison, bored by routine work and despised by the military officers around him, Clive played cards. On a bad night he charged a bullying major with cheating; handled himself with no skill, but with honor, in the pistolling duel that followed; and demonstrated his discriminating intelligence by placing blame for the incident on the red-coated spectators rather than the red-coated cheater. To perfect Clive's motivations, Browning added some details not to be found in true accounts of the event. Nicely contrasting with this whiskyish tale is "Pan and Luna," a poem which handsomely balances fleshly lubricity with delicate charm, all in the context of a Greek myth suggested by some inconsequential lines of Virgil. The innocent Luna is shown commencing her night's journey naked, glistening, and "orbed":

> Orbed—so the woman-figure poets call
> Because of rounds on rounds—that apple-shaped
> Head which its hair binds close into a ball
> Each side the curving ears—that pure undraped
> Pout of the sister paps—that——Once for all
> Say, her consummate circle thus escaped
> With its innumerous circlets, sank absorbed
> Safe in the cloud—O naked moon full-orbed.

She has sought cover in vain; the "coy-caressing stuff/Curdles about her"; and the "Maid-Moon" becomes "clasped around and caught/By rough red Pan." The paradox lies in the fact that the "Girl-moon" was betrayed and caught "bruised to the breast of Pan" through her virtue—" by just her attribute/Of unmatched modesty." In its combination of charm, sensuality, and hardness of thought, "Pan and Luna" transcends all the other poems in the Second Series of *Dramatic Idyls.*

   Attached by some ambivalent typography to "Pan and Luna," or possibly to the whole volume, is a ten-line observation beginning "Touch him ne'er so lightly, into song he broke." This cryptic piece, later increased by some lines beginning "Thus I wrote in London, musing on my betters," is most acceptably explained as a defense of Browning's own ruggedness and depth as opposed to "sweetness" and "ease":

> Rock's the song-soil rather, surface hard and bare:
> Sun and dew their mildness, storm and frost their rage,
> Vainly both expend,—few flowers awaken there:
> Quiet in its cleft broods—what the after age
> Knows and names a pine, a nation's heritage.

Considerable speculation about which poets Browning would put in which category has ensued. He unbelievably excluded himself as the rugged rock-bred "pine," saying once that Dante was the only poet intended. Swinburne and the lost god Shelley have been suggested as the routinely oversweet opposite, but Browning never named a name for that category.

VI   Jocoseria

   The ten "gay*ish* and gray*ish*" pieces gathered in *Jocoseria* (1883) begin prettily and end good-humoredly. "Wanting is—What?" opens the volume with a description of a world in which everything is physically lovely, but "blank" at center, and is awaiting the single element, a lover, which will form the universal nucleus. Its matching poem, "Never the Time and the Place," more specifically calls for the reunion of lovers separated by death. The speaker, clearly Browning, makes interesting use of dreams and reveries in which hostility and malice oppose the longed-for meeting. Doubt haunts him; dreams scare him. Time, place, and loved one may as easily coalesce in the narrow grave as in the "magic of May" which would make a more desirable background. This poem may have been intended for the epilogue to *Jocoseria* but, if so, was supplanted by the spoofing little anecdote called "Pambo." In this ultimate final word, a student, on the advice of a professor, spends his life trying to construe the first verse of Psalm 39, to wit "I said I will look to my ways that I with my tongue offend not." The Student is Browning; the Professor, literary criticism; the tongue, poetry—and Browning jocularly promises to try not to offend.

"Cristina and Monaldeschi," "Mary Wollstonecraft and Fuseli," and "Donald" has each its somewhat historical story to tell. Queen Cristina, after abdicating the throne of Norway, takes Count Monaldeschi for her equerry officer and secret lover. Finding some weaknesses in his love of her, the queen has him shrived and killed. Browning handles the story in unflurried stanzas spoken with regal calm by the lady herself. The second poem of the group again presents a female monologist, the writer and reformer Mary Wollstonecraft, Mary Shelley's mother, who vainly tries to explain in the poem how she has slaved at philosophy and the arts in hope of winning the love of the painter and critic Fuseli. "Donald" is perhaps more interesting for its frame than for the story within the frame. The story grimly attacks blood-sports by telling of a historic encounter between a young man and a great Scottish stag, of their apparently mutual decision to avoid molestation, and of the compulsive treachery of the man ("sportsman first, man after") whichs results in death for the animal and in maiming and beggary for the man. The sprightlier frame-plot renders "a band from Oxford/The oldest of whom was twenty," all drinking happily in a country inn, telling sportsman's lies, and encouraging each other to think that outdoors gunnery gives a man strength and character. By the end of the long inner story they are too drunk to understand either the events or the moral.

In all of these tales Browning took great liberties with his sources. In the three stories proceeding from Jewish legend, he felt even more free to embellish. "Solomon and Balkis," the best of these, tells how the accidental appearance of the "Ineffable Name" (which enforces truth-telling) causes the wisest man in the world to admit that his motivation is vanity rather than love of wisdom, and causes Balkis, Queen of Sheba, to admit (laughing and kissing him) that she has come on her famous visit not to hear his wisdom but to experience his lovemaking. "Adam, Lilith, and Eve" curiously enjambes ancient tale and modern possibility. Frightened by a shattering lightning-bolt, the two earliest females confess the truth about their feelings for Adam. Lilith has pretended to scorn Adam while really adoring him; Eve has wished for somebody else and, by mating with Adam, has "unlocked Hell's gate." After hearing both uncomfortable confessions, Adam wisely elects to consider that both women are joking.

"Jochanin Hakkadosh" is longer than the other two poems on Jewish subjects, and also more demanding, since Browning ornamented his rather simple narrative with a jumble of allusions to obscure data in Jewish writings and tradition. Its hero Jochanin, a scholar dying in his eighty-ninth year, is given five short increments of life by the loving sacrifice of equal time by five friends. Ever a scholar, he hopes to make discoveries by fusing these other lives with his own. His one success occurs in the final fusion, which is with a small child. From this impregnation he comes to the ecstatic state of "ignorance confirmed through knowledge," and he attains the capacity to resolve contradictions much as had Rabbi ben Ezra in Browning's poem of twenty years before. A group of three sonnets made up of the most preposterous legends in the Talmud concludes this resolute jumble.

"Ixion," though both Classical and mythological, most forcefully espouses a conviction of Browning's about God and man. The final disaster of the formerly mortal hero Ixion began with his being invited by the god Zeus to a divine banquet, where he is tricked into presenting himself as a lover to Zeus's wife Hera. For punishment he is made immortal and lashed to a wheel on which he must spin in torment forever. In form, the poem is a monologue in long lines with downturning feminine endings meant to show pain and despondency. However, Ixion's opinions remain sharp and vigorous. Zeus's evil trick only symbolizes the enormous wrongs which Zeus does to all mankind. Ixion's argument moves on to the position that Zeus made man only to torment and kill him, and still on to the harsher position that Zeus makes some men immortal (he instances Tantalus, Sisyphus, and himself) in order to torment and destroy them through eternity:

Flesh that he fashioned with sense of the sea and the sky
    and the ocean,
Framed should pierce to the star, fitted to pore on the plant,—
All, for a purpose of hate, re-framed, re-fashioned, re-fitted
Till, consummate at length,—lo the employment of sense!
Pain is mere minister now to the soul once pledged to her pleasure.

But Browning, or Ixion, is not finished. The concept of Zeus (or any name for God) as a creation of man himself is succeeded by the familiar concept of "a Purity all-unobstructed" to which man continually aspires. Such an "influence, high over Hell" may "turn to a rapture/Pain," and may blend "despair's murk mists ... in a rainbow of hope." Such thinking parallels that of Shelley, especially in *Prometheus Unbound*, but in other respects the poems have little in common. Browning is said to have wept when he read "Ixion" to F. J. Furnivall, his good friend and a founder of the Browning Society. Its scheme is perhaps too compact and intellectual to cause others to weep, but in all-around merit it is surely one of the finest poems to be found among those of his declining years.

CHAPTER 12

The End of Man and Poet

I *How Many Brownings?*

DURING the 1880's, trans-Atlantic society was so-
lidifying its routines of London "season" and Italian
"off-season" with the additional possibilities of France and
Switzerland in certain kinds of weather. Browning, now a
celebrated member of that society, lived much on ships and
trains, terraces and piazzas. The women with whom he continued to form intimacies tended to be older and richer than
before. Three of these women, Clara Bloomfield-Moore,
Katherine Bronson, and his son's wife Fannie Coddington,
American heiresses all, were closest to him in his sunset years.
At Rome, Savoy, Nice, Venice, and at last his adored old city
of Asolo, where Pippa had long since passed, he and the
devoted Sarianna lived in their houses and ate at their tables.
His health and vigor persisted as he approached and passed
his seventieth year. Angry outbursts still came and went. Carlyle and Edward Fitzgerald died, leaving private letters which,
when duly published, traduced characteristics of his lost wife
and of himself. One response of his was the publication of
a transcendently ugly sonnet against "Fitz"; another was the
systematic destruction of his own family letters and other personalia.

But towards himself Browning felt generally forgiving and
even complacent. As was to be shown in *Ferishtah's Fancies*
and elsewhere, he had completed his retreat from responsibilities of a social or political nature, even towards his own
country. In a well-known sonnet called "Why I Am a Liberal,"
he exposed a liberalism frozen into irrelevance forty years
earlier. In his poetry, some characteristic features such as willfully ugly prosody, one-image love lyricism, and pledges to
the dead, continued to appear; but his final three volumes
were totally unlike one another and expressed the writer's

160

unabated struggle to say the final word as strongly and truly
as ever.

As early as 1877, Henry James, still young and not yet
Europeanized, decided that Browning's character possessed
two personae with a deep chasm between them. "Evidently
there are two Brownings, an esoteric and an exoteric," he wrote
home to his sister. "The former never peeps out into society
and the latter has not a ray of suggestion of *Men and Women*."[1]
This impression was reinforced over the years, until in 1892,
after the poet's death, James was able to shape it into his
novelette *The Private Life*. There Browning is thinly disguised
as a brilliant original novelist, Clare Vaudrey, who as a social
being is "sound," "second-rate," and often "coarse." "I never
found him anything but loud and cheerful and copious," says
James's narrator; "and I never ceased to ask myself, in this
particular loud, sound, normal, hearty presence, all so assertive
and so whole, all bristling with prompt responses and expected
opinions and usual views . . . what lodgement, on such premises, the rich proud genius one adored could ever have con-
trived." James's view was not his alone; but if the wealthy
transients whom Browning had chosen as his friends noticed
the dichotomy, they did not seem to mind.

II *Ferishtah's Fancies*

Though cast in an antique Oriental mode, *Ferishtah's
Fancies* (1884) contains a higher proportion of modern and
personal thinking than any earlier volume of Browning's. In
form, it is mainly a set of twelve blank-verse monologues and
dialogues featuring Ferishtah, a dervish or Rabbi of Ishpahan.
Its first discourse, "The Eagle," appears to recur to a youthful
period in which Browning was both choosing a career and
reading some Persian philosophic fables; but most of the work
was done during the latter half of 1883, while the poet basked
in the approval of the Bloomfield-Moore and Bronson estab-
lishments in Venice and in the Italian Alps. Originally the
"fancies" had thematic titles like "Belief," "Pain," Incarnation"—titles which, with the pervasive complacency which
infects almost the whole work, suggests the simultaneous laxity
and fervor often brought to such themes in such circles. The
popularity of the limber philosophy of the book, and of the
mock-profound oriental rag-tags with which Browning covered

its evasions, was attested by quick calls for a second and third edition.

The "Prologue," the "Epilogue," the first "fancy," and some of the love lyrics which are appended to the intellectual efforts escape the routine answer-making which prevails elsewhere. In the "Prologue," Browning explains how, in some Italian cookery, "birdlings" are encased in sage leaf and again in plain bread before actual baking. The eater then bites through "food" and "piquancy" before reaching the true meat which governs the situation. "So with your meat, my poem," says the gourmand-author, once for all dropping the "dramatic" role of a man about to speak the mind of some other man. The first regular poem, "The Eagle," explains the decision of a forest-dwelling youth to leave self-contemplative obscurity to attempt a dedicated public career. Most of the twelve love-lyrics pick up main ideas from the discourses which they follow and apply these to Browning's relationships after the death of Elizabeth Barrett. Mrs. Bloomfield-Moore, a person always excited by Browning, was doubly excited by his responding to her talk of a "soul-love" extant between them with a lyric beginning "Not with the Soul, Love," and arguing the require-ment of sensual and physical passion, "Sense quenching Soul."[2] These love poems were quickly set to music, and several enjoyed long popularity as sheet-music for the parlor piano and the sentimental voice.

Not without some back-reference and overlapping, Ferishtah-Browning tries to confine each discourse to a single lesson or theme. Four poems—"The Melon Seller," "The Fam-ily," "Mihrab Shah," and "A Camel Driver"—handle varia-tions on the themes of pain and evil. In "A Camel Driver," Ferishtah accepts the proposition that men must punish one another for transgressions, but rejects the proposition that God, either on earth or in an after-life, must do the same. The good-ness of life and the propriety of gratitude are argued in "Two Camels," "Cherries," "Plot Culture," and the oddly named "A Bean Stripe: also Apple-Eating." In "Cherries" and "Plot Culture," Ferishtah teaches his scholars to accept good things (here a fruit breakfast and his own daughter's caresses) with gratitude and modesty. In "Two Camels," the ascetic way of life is flatly repudiated, much as it had been in "The Eagle." Man is to enjoy every possible sweetness and comfort and to feel guiltless among every inequity—for, like a self-starved camel, a self-starved man cannot serve others (or serve God) with suitable strength and efficiency.

"A Bean-Stripe: also Apple-Eating," the longest of the "fancies," presents a warm debate between Ferishtah and a dogged and resolute rival, their difference being whether good or evil preponderates in men's lives. The rival philosopher was perhaps Carlyle, towards whose mocking memory Browning continued to be cross. Ferishtah assumes a victory for the life-is-good opinion, but with arguments which would fail to move any person not previously convinced. "Shah Abbas," "The Sun," and "A Pillar at Sebzehvah" all deal with epistemology, especially in matters of belief and doubt. In each of these poems, Ferishtah presents healthy belief as the product of will and desire (combined as "love") rather than of knowledge proceeding from facts or logic. That knowledge changes in each generation is a compelling reason, he argues, to doubt its basic utility. Man should therefore "wholly distrust" knowledge and just "as wholly" trust "love allied to ignorance." So he holds in "A Pillar." In "The Sun," Ferishtah applies the plan to the incarnation of God in Jesus and to other stories impossible to believe in if we depend upon reason and evidence rather than upon love.

By 1884 such arguments represented "routine thinking," a term used by George Woodberry in an otherwise favorable review in the *Atlantic Monthly*.[3] They were luckily transcended in the "Epilogue" in which Browning sadly proposed that opposite views may be as necessary and sound as the cheerful views he has been espousing. Using the moon-metaphor he loved, he acknowledged that the "irridescent splendor" which had blessed him might not be available in the experience of every man. His cosmos has contained "wonder after wonder"—

> Only, at heart's utmost joy and triumph, terror
> Sudden turns the blood to ice; a chill wind disencharms
> All the late enchantment! What if all be error—
> If the halo raised round my head were, Love, thine arms?

That is, perhaps only the lucky accident of a fulfilling love has permitted him to be happy and hopeful. Persons not so lucky would be permitted—what? The expression of so frightening a doubt at the end of so cheerful a volume speaks conclusively for the integrity, if not the consistency, of Browning's thinking.

III   Parleyings with Certain People

Early in 1886 the journal *Critic* noted that Browning, "dreading his future biographer," had "just destroyed the whole of his letters to his father and family, every one of which had been preserved with paternal care." It was rumored, on the other hand, that Browning was writing some autobiographical work of his own.[4] In the following year, when *Parleyings with Certain People of Importance in Their Day* was published, few literary men recognized its connection with the hoped-for autobiography. In reality, the nostalgic bookishness of the volume, as well as the authors used in it, give it the most intimate connection with the long hours of solitary reading and the cheerful hours of father-son book talk in the library in Camberwell. Its system is to reveal its author through the author's addresses to his subjects. With an ingenuity as fresh as ever, Browning thus biographized himself in the second and third persons of grammar, avoiding the dangerous first.

The full title Browning attached to his book was a whimsical version of its table of contents. He called it *Parleyings with Certain People of Importance in their Day: to wit: Bernard Mandeville, Daniel Bartoli, George Bubb Doddington, Francis Furini, Gerard de Lairesse, and Charles Avison. Introduced by a Dialogue between Apollo and the Fates; and Concluded by Another Between John Fust and his Friends.* The two "Dialogues" are formed as five-line stanzas through which the separate speeches cut and chop, but the seven actual "Parleyings" are written in pentameter verse rhyming generally in open couplets that are often reminiscent of Dryden. Browning's forensic stragegy is to draw his people who lived long before into contexts of general importance in 1887, a year given to Victoria's Golden Jubilee and to reflections and evaluations of every kind. The book is, therefore, not merely an intellectual Life, but an intellectual Life and Times. Its "Apollo" and "John Fust" terminals emphasize the literary profession of its author.

To readers of the first edition in 1887, the most interesting of the seven Parleyings were those with Bernard Mandeville

and George Bubb Doddington. Browning who had read Mandeville's *Fable of the Bees* in childhood but not since, managed
to misconstrue its arguments very badly. What was of appeal
was not his concern with Mandeville, however, but his concern
with his "parlous friend," the recently demised Thomas Carlyle. Rightly or wrongly, Mandeville was called upon to help
Browning confute Carlyle's dour view of life in which "Craft
foils rectitude,/Malignity defeats benificence." Between them,
Browning and Mandeville devote ten pages to the metaphoric
and "take case" rebuttals which by now dominated the processes of Browning's mind.

George Bubb Doddington was an eighteenth-century political animal of no standing or success, and Browning used him,
through his published *Diary*, to illustrate the habits which
keep men out of office. The real mission of this Parleying was to
attack the more recently dead Benjamin Disraeli, a man whom
Browning had hated for many years. Politicians like Doddington, as Browning tells the man himself, fail to get office because
of their basic similarity to the voters they wish to cheat and
the superiors they wish to placate. To get and keep power,
he argues, a man needs to command the awe which comes
from some separating quality, plus a way of suggesting some
special relationship to the occult or supernatural. Disraeli's
success had developed, says Browning to Doddington, from
a subtle redoubling of irrational images. He had separated
himself from other politicians by deliberately seeming to be
callous and dishonest, and he had connected himself to the
supernatural by pretending a secret knowledge and control
of any given situation. Doddington had been an understand-
able member of the community; but, as Disraeli is made to
say,

> I pretend
> No such community with men. Perpend
> My key to domination! Who would use
> Man for his pleasure needs must introduce
> The element that awes men.

Of Disraeli, Browning said in his own voice that there must
be "something . . . uncanny in the—quack?" It is an honest
question mark; for, though he hated Disraeli, Browning never

really professed to understand his character or his role in British politics.

With the speeches directed toward Avison, Smart, and Bartoli, Browning sketched in some of his profoundest thinking about the fine arts. Avison, an organist of Newcastle in the eighteenth century, had swum into the ken of the boy Browning through his tune "Grand March" and his book *An Essay on Musical Expression* (1752). Recalling the excitement with which he had encountered the "little book/And large tune," Browning is led to argue that music is the best equipped of all arts to record the permanent passions of mankind; but that also, because of its style-shifts, it is the least capable of presenting them successfully over a long period. The musical notations of Avison's "Grand March," with new lyrics honoring the regicide Pym, conclude this rather ostentatious poem. The "Parleying with Christopher Smart" begins with an architectural metaphor. Browning envisages a palace the many rooms of which are furnished tastefully and expensively, but remain banal and uninteresting—all but one, a brilliantly decorated and furnished chapel room that conveys "beauty with magnificence" and presents "from floor to roof one evidence/Of how far earth may rival heaven." The banal palace represents eighteenth-century verse, and the brilliant chapel is the "Song to David" written in a madhouse by Christopher Smart and cherished by Browning from his early youth. The Parleying emphasizes motivation rather than inspiration, and quickly drifts from the values of Smart to those of some modern poets, especially Swinburne. Smart has worked within a self-dedication both religious and didactic; but Swinburne and other young men of the Esthetic movement propose to exploit the world's beauties and their own talents only "for art's sake." Browning concludes that art must occur within the context of values beyond the mere artifact.

In "Parleying with Gerard de Lairesse" Browning attacked the decorative use of ancient fable and, by expansion, all Hellenism in art. De Lairesse was a late seventeenth-century painter who, upon losing his eyesight, wrote a book entitled *The Art of Painting in all its Branches*. An English translation dated 1778 was in the Browning library. In 1874, Browning reported that he had "read this book more often and with greater delight when I was a child than any other, and still remember the main of it for the good I seem to have got from the prints and the wonderful text."[5] By 1885, his opinion had changed. De Lairesse had believed in the pictorial value of ancient literature and myth; had wanted all paintings, even landscapes, to be as full of classical figures and allusions as possible; and had tried to refer every esthetic and technical question to the rule and practice of the ancients. Browning, who was beginning to notice and resent the Classical orientation of such younger rivals as Matthew Arnold and Swinburne, countered by repeating, ostensibly against de Lairesse, his own previous theories about the deadness, because of its perfection, of Greek art.

In this Parleying he was very exact. Two chapters of de Lairesse's book had comprised an imaginary "walk" in which the master pointed out how beauties of nature might be embellished by thickly overset figures from the ancient myths. Most of Browning's poem is presented as a rival "walk" in which different, often comic, systems of embellishment are proposed. From this "fooling," he turned to open preachment: who "seeks fire" in the Classics "finds ashes." The world's "young significance is all to learn:/The dead Greek lore lies buried in the urn." The poem concludes with another outcry against pessimism:

> By proved potency that still
> Makes perfect, be assured, come what come will,
> What once lives never dies—what here obtains
> To a beginning, has no end,—still gains
> And never loses aught: when, where, or how
> Lies in Law's lap. What's death then?

And so on, with a noticeable skew towards contradiction of the previous argument. Browning's large observations had approached stereotype, and he no longer checked their cogency in particular situations.

The parleyings with Daniel Bartoli and Francis Furini depart from the standard by simplicity on the one hand and complexity on the other. Bartoli, a seventeenth-century Jesuit whose major book, *De' Simboli Transportati al Morale,* was edited in London by Browning's tutor in Italian, had long been cherished by the poet as a model of Italian style. Bartoli's interest lay with the moral instruction to be drawn from lives of saints, and Browning counters with a love story drawn from secular history and embodying his characteristic lady-in-distress motif—and Bartoli hardly enters the poem at all.

The 616 lines of "Parleying with Francis Furini" make it twice as long as other poems in the book. Furini was a painter famous for his devotion to "painting women . . ./Just as God made them," until, at forty, he renounced painting and entered the priesthood. Most of his paintings still hung in Florence when the Brownings lived there, and his story had been told by the moralistic Baldinucci, from which "scruple-splitting, sickly-sensitive,/Mild moralist" Browning got it. When the *Parleyings* was written, Penini Browning was under critical attack for his own almost exclusive interest in painting the nude, and the poem thus begins as a defense of both painters against their most notable critics, Bartoli against Baldinucci, and Penini Browning against the gallery executive J. C. Horsley, on the issue of what the poet called "God's best of beauteous and magnificent/Revealed to earth, the naked female form." Browning follows anticipated lines of defense by stressing the sacredness of the flesh and the difference between artistic and sexual desires concerning it, and then counters with a bitter vituperation against the prurient criticism which sees matters otherwise. The poem then follows Furini into priestly concerns, and has its say about Hope, Doubt, and Death before culminating in a forensic display aimed against the evolutionists' view of human development—a view Browning thought Furini would have thought too narrow. At long last Browning ends where he began, with nudes, and in particular with a painting of Joan of Arc about to bathe, a huge new canvas by his son Penini.

The prologue and epilogue of *Parleyings* are among the swiftest in movement of all Browning's poems. Both are all dialogue. "Apollo and the Fates" refers back to *Balaustion's Adventure* and to an off-stage incident in the *Alkestes* of Euripides, and has for its main interest the contrast between the hopeful and idealistic young god Apollo and the three fatal sisters who rule men's lives. One of its passages, when Apollo has made the scrawny beldames drunk and all four commence dancing and singing together, is a prime example of the comic-grotesque; and the mocking "tra-la-la" and "ha-ha-ha" with which the Fates finally brush away the poet-god's faith in humanity are still disconcerting. "John Fust and His Friends" similarly falls into the mode of comic-grotesque. The dialogue combines the Faust of the legend with the Fust of typographical history, and it offers some generally negative observations about both men and books. In their liveliness, cynicism, and grimly humorous tone, the two dialogues nicely set off the moralizing tendencies of the seven poems they enclose.

IV   Asolando: Fancies and Facts

Asolando, Browning's thirty-fifth volume, seems almost to have been written as a summary of his poetic career. It was published on December 12, 1889, the day of his death. Its title refers to the Asolo of *Sordello* and *Pippa Passes*, a city he loved above all others, and to his most common pairing of contraries. Although all but a few were written during the last two years of his life, its thirty-one poems maintain a higher standard than any collection of his since the *Dramatis Personae* of a quarter-century before, and offer in scope and variety a microcosm of all the interests he had followed throughout his life. Nor was Browning to fail to know the reward due to a perfect sampler perfectly timed; for, while lying in his son's palace in Venice, perishing in the midst of admiration, love, luxury, and art, he learned by telegraph that *Asolando* had earned handsome reviews and was selling out its first edition on its first day.

The poems in *Asolando* may be, with a little violence, sectioned into four groups. The first of these is made up of love lyrics, some general enough for application to any or all of the women in his life, and others easily applicable to individual women. "Now," "Humility," "Poetics," "Summum Bonum," and "A Pearl, a Girl," celebrate the possibility of love matches perhaps fleeting but so vital as to subsume all other experience:

> The moment eternal—just that and no more—
> When ecstasy's utmost we clutch at the core
> While cheeks burn, arms open, eyes shut and lips meet.

In "White Witchcraft," a short dialogue partly drawn from Virgil, Browning fancies his lady turned into a fox ("shy, wild stealer of the grapes"), and himself turned into a toad whose

wrinkled skin and despised shape the lady will ignore in favor
of his "eyes that follow mine—love lasts there anyhow."

In sharply naturalistic contrast is the longer love poem "Inap-
prehensiveness," a cameo of two figures against an Asolan
landscape. The woman (certainly Mrs. Bronson) speaks
intensely about the sky, the mosses, the ruined castle, and
John Ruskin; but the man throbs and writhes with suppressed
passions:

> Oh fancies that may be, oh facts that are!
> What of a wilding? By you stands, and may
> So stand unnoticed until Judgment Day,
> One who, if once aware that your regard
> Claims what his heart holds,—woke as from its sward
> The flower, the dormant passion, so to speak—
> Then what a rush of life would startling wreak
> Vengeance on your inapprehensive stare.

In "Dubiety," tracing the source of a gauzy autumn comfort
which has "disarmed the world," thus permitting "Out-
side/Quiet and peace: inside, nor blame,/Nor want, nor wish,"
the speaker finds the source not in a dream or dharma but
in a simple memory of a woman, undoubtedly Elizabeth Barrett, as she leaned over "to feel for my brow where a kiss
might fall." "Speculative," a more routine love poem, presents
the dead wife as equivalent to the improved "Man, Nature,
Art" to be found perhaps in the "new life" others hope to
find after death. Had she lived, "earth's old life" would have
served as well.

Seven poems in *Asolando* retell events from the history of
ages long past. In "Rosny," a sinister little ballad for two voices,
the death of a "love-maddened" participant in an illicit love
affair is adjudged a good thing after all. "Muckle-mouth Meg"
records with charm a wry love story from the family history
of Sir Walter Scott. Of "The Cardinal and the Dog," "The
Pope and the Net," and "The Bean Feast," the first is interesting for its date of 1842 and its source in Wanley's *Wonders
of the Little World*, that strange childhood source of so many
of Browning's occult fantasies; and the second and third for
their chiseled presentation of two radically opposed characteristics of the sixteenth-century historical Pope Sixtus the
Fifth.

More serious as art are the longer historical narratives
"Ponte del Angelo Venice" and "Beatrice Signorini." "Ponte
del Angelo" very amusingly retells the legend of a greedy Renaissance lawyer whose one servant, a great ape, is actually
the Devil on watch to capture his soul on the first night he
omits to pray to the Virgin. Browning took the story from a
contemporary book about Venice, Tassini's *Curiosita Ve-
neziane* (1863), but sought to give it dignity by attributing it
to "Father Boverio.../In his Annals" (1632-39), the book
from which Tassini had taken it. "Beatrice Signorini," a narrative of 352 lines delightfully rhymed as open couplets, is pil-
laged from Browning's reliable old source and enemy, "Block-
head Baldinucci." This very interesting triangle in this snatch
of art history consists of the Baroque artist Romanelli, his soft-
seeming wife Beatrice Signorini ("My gentle consort with the
milk for blood"), and Artemisia Gentilischi, a professional
painter still well known for the nudes and fruits she liked best
to paint. Finding his wife insipid and colorless, Romanelli
transfers his admiration to his unresponding colleague Artemisia, pays for the transgression when his wife drops her
mousy disguise to rip up the portrait of Artemisia which is his
dearest possession, and is so pleased by the change of emotional tone as to keep his love within his marriage forever after.
Browning calls the story a "petty incident," but took pains in
drawing up his three main characters. In her combination of
charm, virtue, and professional attitude, Artemisia is especially delightful.

As Browning's last word to those with ears to hear, *Asolando*
necessarily contained a number of admonitory poems. The
comparative indifference to human suffering which was a
necessary ingredient to his philosophic optimism never
extended to animals; and "Arcades Ambo" and "The Lady
and the Painter" attack, respectively, vivisection and the use
of bird wings in millinery. "Flute-Music," a gladsome dialogue
between a realistic girl and an imaginative man, tests facts
against fancy in bizarre stanzas made up of twelve short lines
apiece and studded with wild rhythms and mad rhymes—all
in harmony, so to speak, with the disharmonious "tootlings
hoarse and husky" of a beginning flautist. The poem "Which"
shows three noblewomen playfully contesting "who judges
best/In esteeming the love of a man." The first desires her

lover to be a dutiful citizen; the second wants an active cavalier who, for her sake, will earn "wounds—each wide mouth to my mercy appealing"; and the third will have any "wretch" who in his need will "stretch/Arms to me his sole saviour." The fashionable snuff-taking Abbé who plays judge unexpectedly endorses the choice of the third woman, for he feels that the desperate third man is "very like what perhaps gains God's preference." The poem "Reverie" moves from a familiar statement of religious belief to that series of arguments against scientific and literary doubters which so crowded the pages of *Ferishtah's Fancies,* and might be called "Reasoning" as easily as "Reverie."

Though supposedly the companion-piece to "Reverie," the fantasy-poem "Rephan" has little affinity to it. "Rephan" is a peculiar amalgam of Browning's childhood reading in evangelistic science-fiction, his mature theorizing on his favorite dilemma of complete and incomplete, and the swiftly exact versification of his later years. The unnamed speaker in the poem has formerly inhabited another planet, "the star Rephan," on which "absolute bliss" is the perpetual condition of existence:

> No want—whatever should be, is now:
> No growth—that's change, and change comes—how
> To royalty born with crown on brow?
>
> Nothing begins—so needs to end:
> Where fell it short at first? Extend
> Only the same, no change can mend.

By some process which the speaker cannot explain, he finds the static perfection of Rephan intolerable: "And I yearned for no sameness, but difference/In thing and thing, that should shock my sense/With a want of worth in them all." The familiar subthemes enter the poem swiftly. "Not reach—aspire but never attain"; "To suffer, did pangs bring the loved one bliss"; to "Burn and not smoulder, win by worth,/Not rest content with a wealth that's dearth." At last the speaker is freed from the living death of a perfected life—"Thou art past Rephan, thy place be Earth."

In a totally different way than "Rephan," without fantasy,

the poem "Imperante Augusto Natus Est" is also a worthy replay. Like the "Cleon" and "Kharshish" of decades before, it presents a segment of the pagan world in bewildering first contact with Christian possibilities. The speaker is a Roman gentleman who, with his friend Publius, sits waiting for his turn to enter the marble baths. Since Christ is still in his obscure infancy, and they have less hard data to work with than Cleon or Karshish, they must make their ironies by misinterpretations of myth and prophecy. Coarse, gossipy, and self-centered, the two Romans are among the most vivid of all the characters whom Browning causes to reveal themselves through the otherwise-intended discourse of dramatic monologue.

V Asolando: *Arrival and Departure*

The remaining poems of *Asolando* are personal and reminiscent. The "Prologue," which is dated "Asolo, September 6, 1889," combines praise of the city with an explication of the second half of the title, "Fancies and Facts." Once in his youth, Browning says, the poet found Asolo and all its environs "involved with alien glow—/His own soul's iris bow." Now he sees "the naked very thing," and the thrill has gone. His recompense, like Wordsworth's in poems of similar orientation, is the improved intellectual skill with which he may "unlink . . ./Fancy from fact." The poem "Development," meant as a long metaphoric argument against hasty intellectualizations of popular religion, has become famous for its secondary function of revealing the educational process administered through "slow and sure degrees" in Camberwell by Robert Browning's father.

The four poems entitled "Bad Dreams" take us into a quite different world. They feature a mutually disconsolate man and woman whose dreams offer the richest analytic experience since the early "Women and Roses." The most interesting, perhaps, is "Bad Dreams II," which begins with a sordid "army of haters" who dance in pairs under a great dome:

> Strange ball
> Hands and feet plighting troth,
> Yet partners enforced and loth.
> Of who danced there, no shape
> Did I recognise: thwart, perverse

> Each grasped each, past escape
>   In a whirl of weary or worse:
>   Man's sneer met woman's curse.

The dreamer gradually makes his way to a chapel, a high throne, and a "vestured priest" who seems to preside over the nightmare sport in the horrible ballroom. When a veiled worshipper appears, she is the man's mate; and her appearance in the chapel is so unacceptable that the dream lurches and breaks apart. Waking in the woman's presence, the man is quarrelsome and inquisitional; and the woman responds with falsely intended inconsequentialities. "Bad Dreams IV" takes place in a graveyard, and projects the guilt of the speaker through the voice of a "slim ghost" who sits contemplating her own tombstone and remembering an overcritical "strong stern man my lover." Browning's wavering between dissatisfaction with himself as a husband and dissatisfaction with Elizabeth Barrett as a wife, a wavering often recorded in poems, and noted several times in this book, is most convincingly recorded in this sequence of "Bad Dreams" poems.

In an ideal world, the woman addressed with great intimacy in the first stanza of the "Epilogue to *Asolando*" would be the ghostly Elizabeth Barrett; but, in fact, she is probably Mrs. Bronson. The other three stanzas comprise Browning's estimate of his own life and character. He assigns himself a high evalutation:

> One who never turned his back but marched breast forward,
>   Never doubted clouds would break,
> Never dreamed, though right were worsted, wrong would triumph,
>   Hold we fall to rise, are baffled to fight better,
>   Sleep to wake.

In Venice, reading proofs of the "Epilogue" shortly before his death, Browning told the two women sitting near him that the quoted stanza "almost seems like bragging, and as if I ought to cancel it." But then, nerving himself, he added "It's the simple truth; and, as it's true, it shall stand."[6] The message of the "Epilogue" is tired and the expression undoubtedly strident. Still we may like the test which allowed it to stand uncancelled.

CHAPTER 13

What Browning Made

R OBERT Browning was a great writer in a society so thoroughly book-oriented as to regard great writers as great men. He was revered as a prophet in an age which liked prophesy, and renowned for a romantic love-marriage in an age which cherished romantic love. After a shaky beginning, he became the greatest exemplar of middle-class British sturdiness, independence, and decisiveness of character. A thoroughly masculine man, bold in approach, often bullying, he found his largest audiences among women. No writer in history has inspired so many clubs, societies, guilds, and museums dedicated to his fame. And paradoxically, no writer in history has excited so much attention from writers, or been so much imitated by writers, in the generations immediately following his own. More than any poet before or since, he attracted the enthusiastic support of great masses of the reading public, and at the same time the admiration and emulation of his friends and rivals in poetry. Turning from the sheer massiveness of Browning's accomplishment, we may ask about his particular achievements as a public voice, as a general artist and man of letters, and finally as a technical practitioner.

As a public voice, the utterer of truths, beliefs, and speculations important to his generation, he enjoyed an unparalleled success in his own time. In an age of doubt he was regarded as an "optimist" and a believer, in a mechanistic age he was loved as a champion of humanity and the human intellect. As his contemporary Augustine Birrell put it, "He lives in our minds a joint-life with the manifold emotions, the countless joys and sorrows, hopes and fears, doubts and certainties, that course one another, like shadows over the hillside,"[1] and the number of books and articles written to present Browning as comforter of these "manifold emotions" is enormous. But by 1914 or so, the view of Browning as seer and comforter was hardly taken any more. In comparison with the other public voices of his England, say Carlyle, Ruskin, Darwin, J. H. Newman, and Marx, he appears unoriginal, and often even uncourageous. Browning's tendency was always to escape from clear dilemmas by presenting less clear ones; his way of dealing with hard issues was generally to soften them; the "optimism" for which he was praised shone the brighter for its contrast with the intellectual shambles over which it was poised. Speaking of both Browning and Tennyson, F. L. Lucas said, "They seem to me pure poets damaged by being too honored as prophets.... They were led more and more to preach, where they should have sung."[2] In this light we may see Browning not so much as a champion of the Victorian delight in public prophecy, but as a victim and martyr to it.

The shyness and uncertainty which hoarsened Browning's public voice was not in the least characteristic of his professional voice. As a career-oriented man of letters he was vigorous, daring, and independent to the point of arrogance. He took a perverse delight in turning out books which reviewers found "harsh, facetious, ingenious, horrible."[3] His early books *Pauline* and *Sordello* having been trounced by critics and public alike for their roughness, willfulness, and obscurity, he bitterly set himself to making roughness, willfulness, and obscurity acceptable and salable. As we have seen, he liked to mount attacks and counterattacks on critics of his poetry; his response to the whole "goose breed" of reviewers never rose above anger and contempt. He was thus all his life the subject of controversy and argument; he was that rare thing, a newsworthy poet, a fact that helped him greatly in the career side of his work. Today those who read a good deal of the journalism that was lavished on Browning in the nineteenth century will be amused by the frequency with which journalists argued that he could never be a well-known poet. Assertions steadily made about him were that "he makes too great demands on his readers," "he cultivates his weeds rather than his flowers," "the common reader can not read Browning," and—repeated endlessly for forty years, even while Browning's popularity reached avalanche proportions—"he cannot be popular.... He is caviare for the general." There was also good criticism, and a perfectly acceptable amount of enthusiastic criticism, though much of the latter was based on the merits of Browning as a thinker or teacher, not his merits as a poet.

In his work as a practicing technician in the art of poetry he was bold, inventive, and many-sided. Smaller poets of his own time thought of him as a colossal force making for freedom and energy in a Victorian world which seemed censorious and flattening. He was called a "neo-Elizabethan titan," and often compared to Ben Jonson in the qualities of toughness, good humor, and copiousness of invention. Less interested in "thought" and wholly uninterested in "prophecy," poets in the generation following his focused their attention on Browning's language, "cacophany, psychological stress, obscurity, and all."[4] As Rupert Brooke pointed out, no poet before Browning could have begun a poem with the line, "Grrrr————there go, my heart's abhorrence!"[5] The boldness of his statement and copiousness of his useable knowledge impressed other writers. G. H. Palmer, writing in 1918, correctly traced to him "the beginnings of that Naturalism which henceforth, for good or ill, was to flood our poetry."[6] To Ezra Pound and the "tribe of Ezra," a category which included an enormous number of the practicing poets of Britain and America, he was always a hero and a model. "Robert Browning," wrote Pound,

> ... ye old mesmerizer
> Tyin' your meanin' in seventy swadelins,
> One must of needs be a hang'd early riser
> To catch you at worm turning. Holy Odd's bodykins!

Pound's *Cantos* could never have been written without the posthumous encouragement of Browning, and the same may be said for very much, perhaps most, of the poetry of the twentieth century.

The massiveness of Browning's contribution is nicely illustrated by his ability to comfort the religious and speculative troubles of millions of subliterary people the world over, to maintain his starring role and his newsworthiness as a personality, and to give leadership and encouragement to the breed of supermodern poets whose interest was confined to technical aspects of his workmanship. What does the ordinary reader who belongs to none of these groups find in Browning's work today? Browning remains the darling of graduate schools; for the richness, variety, and sheer bulk of the thirty volumes he left behind offer apparently unlimited topics for research and comment. In high schools and undergraduate colleges, a few dozen staple poems are taught and read. Of the long poems, *Pippa Passes* is the joy of some students, though not all; and the favorites among the shorter poems are "My Last Duchess," "Porphyria's Lover," "Youth and Art," "Andrea Del Sarto," and other veterans of the classroom. But Browning is still at his best when read outside of classrooms, on sofas and under trees, with courage and curiosity, in the search for the pleasure that comes with experience.

Notes and References

Chapter One

1. Alexandra Orr, *Life and Letters of Robert Browning* (London, 1891), p. 10.
2. Betty Miller, *Robert Browning: A Portrait* (London, 1952), pp. 4–14.
3. Letter of Benjamin Jowett to Tennyson, 1887. In *Tennyson: A Memoir by His Son* (London: 1897), II, 224.
4. Diary of Alfred Domett, Feb. 7, 1873, quoted in W. H. Griffin and H. C. Minchin, *Life Of Browning* (New York, edn. of 1966), p. 29.
5. Letter to Elizabeth Barrett, Aug. 10, 1845. Printed locations of cited letters may be found in my "Calendar of Letters," in L. N. Broughton, C. S. Northup, and R. B. Pearsall, *Robert Browning: A Bibliography 1830–1950* (New York, 1953 and 1970), pp. 341–402.

Chapter Two

1. Anon. in *Fraser's Magazine*, Dec. 1833; J. S. Mill, in Griffin and Minchin, *Life of Browning;* W. J. Fox, in *Monthly Repository*, April 1833; Joseph Arnould, letter of 1847, in F. G. Kenyon, ed., *Robert Browning and Alfred Domett* (London, 1906), p. 141.
2. W. C. DeVane, *Browning Handbook* (New York, 1955), p. 47.
3. G. K. Chesterton, *Robert Browning* (London, 1903), p. 25.
4. For these and other comments, DeVane, *Handbook*, pp. 85–86; Broughton, Northup, and Pearsall, *Browning Bibliography*, pp. 87–89, and see index; Boyd Litzinger, *Time's Revenges* (Knoxville, 1964), *passim*.
5. Browning's "Advertisement" in the first edition, 1841, later removed.
6. Alexandra Orr, *Browning Handbook* (London, edn. of 1890), p. 55.
7. Letter of Browning to Elizabeth Barrett, April 5, 1846, and other letters on both sides.

Chapter Three

1. W. C. Macready, *Diaries*, ed. W. Toynbee (London, 1912), Nov. 23, 1836.
2. Macready, *Diaries*, Sept. 5, 1839.
3. Alexandra Orr, *Life and Letters* (revised edn., London 1910), p. 97.

4. Letter of Browning to Macready, Dec. 1840.
5. Quoted in Griffin and Minchin, *Life*, p. 115.
6. Anon. in *Athenaeum*, April 30, 1855.

Chapter Four

1. *Dramatic Lyrics* (1st edn., London, 1842), p. [2].
2. Anon in *Spectator*, Dec. 10, 1842.
3. Letter of Browning to F. A. Ward, Feb. 18, 1845; letter of Elizabeth Barrett to Browning, Nov. 15, 1845; John Ruskin in *Modern Painters* (London, 1856), IV, 380.
4. Letter of Elizabeth Barrett to Browning, May 26, 1846, and repeated in other letters.

Chapter Five

1. Letter of Browning to W. W. Story, June 11, 1854.
2. Joseph Milsand, in *Revue Contemporaire* (Paris), Sept. 15, 1856. Quoted at more length in DeVane, *Handbook*, p. 211.
3. Betty Miller, *Browning: A Portrait*, pp. 145–47.

Chapter Six

1. See Maisie Ward, *Browning and His World* (New York, 1967, 1969), II, 96.
2. Letter of Browning to Ruskin, Dec. 10, 1855.
3. Cardinal Wiseman in his review of *Men and Women*, in *The Rambler*, Jan. 1856.

Chapter Seven

1. Browning's achievement as a father is maturely assessed by Betty Miller in *Browning: A Portrait*, which incorporates much of her earlier article "The Child of Casa Guidi," *Cornhill Magazine*, Spring, 1949.
2. In *Monthly Repository*, May, 1836.
3. Letter of Browning to Julia Wedgwood, Dec. 25, 1864.
4. DeVane, *Browning's "Parleyings"* (New York, 1927), pp. 255–57.

Chapter Eight

1. Letter of Browning to Isa Blagden, Sept. 19, 1864.
2. (Chicago, 1968), pp. 43–46.
3. Anon., review in *Dublin Review*, July, 1869.

Chapter Nine

1. Specifically, Plutarch's *Life of Nicias*.
2. J. A. Symonds, in *Academy*, April 17, 1875.
3. In F. G. Kenyon, ed., *The Works of Robert Browning* (Centenary Edition, London, 1912), VIII, vii.

4. Letter of Browning to J. H. Ingram, Feb. 11, 1876.
5. Quoted in Griffin and Minchin, *Life*, pp. 255–56.
6. Letter of A. C. Swinburne to John Nichol, quoted in Maisie Ward, *Browning and His World*, II, 106.

Chapter Ten

1. J. R. Dennett, in *The Nation*, Sept. 14, 1871.
2. See Broughton, Northup, and Pearsall, *Browning Bibliography*, pp. 114–23, and index.
3. Alexandra Orr, *Handbook*, pp. 150 ff.
4. W. D. Howells, in *Atlantic Monthly*, March, 1876.

Chapter Eleven

1. Letters of Browning to F. J. Furnivall, Jan. 9, 1883; and to J. D. Williams, April 17, 1883.
2. Maisie Ward, *Browning and His World*, II, 158.
3. Betty Miller, *Browning: A Portrait*, pp. 250–52, 259–62.
4. The exchange is explored by Betty Miller in *Browning: A Portrait*, pp. 243–45.
5. F. G. Kenyon in an editorial note to his edition, *The Works of Browning* (London, 1912), IX, xvi.
6. Anon., in *The Pen*, Aug. 7, 1880.
7. Anon., in *Pall Mall Gazette*, July 26, 1880.

Chapter Twelve

1. See Maisie Ward, *Browning and His World*, II, 257–67. "The Private Life" was first published in *Atlantic Monthly*, April, 1892.
2. Amusingly related by Betty Miller, *Browning: A Portrait*, pp. 267–69.
3. George Woodberry, in *Atlantic Monthly*, April, 1885.
4. Anon. in *The Critic*, Jan. 2, 1886, giving *The Academy* as source.
5. Quoted by Griffin and Minchin, *Life*, pp. 9–10, from a copy inscribed by Browning.
6. An anonymous communication called "Browning's Faith," *Pall Mall Gazette*, Feb. 1, 1890. Of the two hearers of the statement, Frances Coddington and Sarianna Browning, the latter is surely the submitter of the communication.

Chapter Thirteen

1. Quoted in Broughton, Northup, and Pearsall, eds., *Browning Bibliography*, p. vii.
2. F. L. Lucas, *Eight Victorian Poets* (Cambridge, 1930), pp. 21–38.
3. Unsigned review in *The Guardian*, Sept. 27, 1876, p. 1280.

4. Richard Burton, "Originality in Literature," *The Dial*, Oct. 16, 1896.

5. Rupert Brooke, in "Browning's Jahrhundertfeier," *International Monatschrift für Wissenschaft* (Berlin), Vol VII (1913), 664.

6. G. H. Palmer, *Formative Types in English Poetry* (Boston, 1918), pp. 271–311.

Selected Bibliography

MANUSCRIPT MATERIALS

Browning's early literary manuscripts are widely scattered, and many are lost. The manuscript of *The Ring and the Book* is in the British Museum Library; manuscripts of all books from *Balaustion's Adventure* through *Parleyings with Certain People* are in the library of Balliol College, Oxford; and the manuscripts of *Dramatis Personae* and *Asolando* are in the Morgan Library, New York.

Other noteworthy manuscript materials are lodged in the Balliol and Bodley Libraries, Oxford; the British Museum; the Victoria and Albert Museum; in the Keats-Shelley House in Rome and in the Biblioteca Nazionale in Florence; in libraries at the universities of Chicago, Illinois, and Texas; at Baylor University, Yale University, and Harvard University; and in the Huntington Library, the Morgan Library, and the Berg Collection of the New York Public Library.

The manuscripts of the magical series of letters which passed between Robert Browning and Elizabeth Barrett in 1845–46 are in the library of Wellesley College.

PRIMARY SOURCES

Listed are books published by Robert Browning as separate units, and the more important of the volumes that contain letters of the poet. A full account of periodical contributions may be found in *Robert Browning, A Bibliography 1830–1950*, compiled by L. N. Broughton, C. S. Northup, and R. B. Pearsall, and listed among the secondary sources below. In the same volume is a Calendar of Letters which sets about 2300 items of Browning's correspondence in chronological order. As the titles of collections show, the letters have been clustered and printed just as they came into the hands of editors. No attempt to organize the mass into a single orderly edition has yet been made.

1. *Browning's Books*

Pauline: A Fragment of a Confession. London: Saunders and Otley, 1833.
Paracelsus. London: Effingham Wilson, 1835.
Strafford: An Historical Tragedy. London: Longman, Rees *et al.*, 1837.

Sordello. London: Edward Moxon, 1840.

Pippa Passes. London: Edward Moxon, 1841, ("Bells and Pome-
    granates" series, No. I).

King Victor and King Charles. London: Edward Moxon, 1842 (BP,
    No, II).

Dramatic Lyrics. London: Edward Moxon, 1842 (BP, No. III).

The Return of the Druses. London: Edward Moxon, 1843 (BP, No.
    IV).

A Blot in the 'Scutcheon. London: Edward Moxon, 1843 (BP, No.
    V).

Columbe's Birthday. London: Edward Moxon, 1844 (BP, No. VI).

Dramatic Romances and Lyrics. London: Edward Moxon, 1845 (BP,
    No. VII).

Luria, and *A Soul's Tragedy.* London: Edward Moxon, 1846 (BP,
    No. VIII and last).

Christmas Eve and *Easter Day.* London: Chapman and Hall, 1850.

Men and Women. London: Chapman and Hall, 1855. Two volumes.

Dramatis Personae. London: Chapman and Hall, 1864.

The Ring and the Book. London: Smith, Elder and Co., 1868 and
    1869. Four volumes, published at one-month intervals.

Balaustion's Adventure, Including a Transcript from Euripides [that
    is, a translation of the *Alcestes* of Euripides]. London: Smith,
    Elder and Co., 1871.

Prince Hohenstiel-Schwangau, Saviour of Society. London: Smith,
    Elder and Co., 1871.

Fifine at the Fair. London: Smith, Elder and Co., 1872.

Red-Cotton Nightcap Country or *Turf and Towers.* London: Smith,
    Elder and Co., 1873.

Aristophanes' Apology, Including a Last Transcript from Euripides
    [That is, a translation of Euripides' *Hercules Furens*], *Being the
    Last Adventure of Balaustion.* London: Smith, Elder and Co.,
    1875.

Pacchiarotto and How he Worked in Distemper, with Other Poems.
    London: Smith, Elder and Co., 1876.

The Agamemnon of Aeschylus. London: Smith, Elder and Co., 1877.

La Saisiaz, and *The Two Poets of Croisic.* London: Smith, Elder
    and Co., 1878.

Dramatic Idyls. London: Smith, Elder and Co., 1879.

Dramatic Idyls, Second Series. London: Smith, Elder and Co., 1880.

Jocoseria. London: Smith, Elder and Co., 1883.

Ferishtah's Fancies. London: Smith, Elder and Co., 1883.

Parleyings with Certain People of Importance in their Day.... Lon-
    don: Smith, Elder and Co., 1887.

Asolando: Fancies and Facts. London: Smith, Elder and Co., 1890
    (actually published Dec. 12, 1889).

2. *Browning's Letters*

The Letters of Robert Browning and Elizabeth Barrett Barrett.
London: Smith, Elder and Co., 1899. Two volumes. New edition,
ed. Elvan Kintner, Cambridge, Mass.: Harvard University Press,
1969. Two volumes.

Robert Browning and Alfred Domett. Ed. by F. G. Kenyon. London:
Smith, Elder and Co., 1906.

Letters of Robert Browning. Collected by T. J. Wise, ed. by T. L.
Hood. New Haven: Yale University Press, 1933.

*Robert Browning and Julia Wedgwood: A Broken Friendship as
Revealed by their Letters.* London: John Murray, 1937.

New Letters of Robert Browning. Ed. by W. C. DeVane and K. L.
Knickerbocker. New Haven: Yale University Press, 1950.

Dearest Isa: Robert Browning's Letters to Isabella Blagden. Austin:
University of Texas Press, 1951.

Letters of the Brownings to George Barrett. Ed. by Paul Landis.
Urbana: University of Illinois Press, 1958.

*Browning to his American Friends: Letters between the Brownings,
the Storys, and James Russell Lowell.* Ed. by Gertrude Reese
Hudson. New York: Barnes and Noble, 1965.

*Learned Lady: Letters from Robert Browning to Mrs. Thomas
Fitzgerald.* Ed. by E. C. McAleer. Cambridge: Harvard University Press, 1966.

SECONDARY SOURCES

The items below are grouped, first, as bibliographical and reference
works, and, second, as general biography and criticism. Only a handful
of the thronging books about Browning are given. A full account
of books and periodical writings is to be found in *Robert Browning:
A Bibliography 1830–1950*, listed below. In the two Browning sections of the *New Cambridge Bibliography of English Literature* (Vol.
III, 1969), both by R. B. Pearsall, the listings after 1950 are made
very complete so as to provide a very full listing from the point
at which the *Bibliography* terminates.

1. *Bibliographies and Reference*

WISE, T. J. *A Complete Bibliography of the Writings of Robert
Browning.* London: privately printed, 1897. Luxury volume
printed "for private subscribers"; lists some manuscripts and
letters as well as printed works.

BROUGHTON, L. N., C. S. NORTHUP, and R. B. PEARSALL. *Robert
Browning: A Bibliography 1830–1950.* Ithaca and London: Cor-
nell University Press, 1953. New edition, New York, Burt Frank-

lin Publishers, 1970. Large general bibliography of works and
ana, with a Calendar of Letters and other special sections.

BROUGHTON, L. N., and B. F. STELTER. *A Concordance to the Poems
of Robert Browning*. Two volumes. New York: G. E. Stechert
and Co., 1924.

ORR, ALEXANDRA. *A Handbook on the Works of Robert Browning*.
London: George Bell and Sons, 1885. "Authorized" handbook
reflecting Browning's criticism of his close friend's criticism of
his work and thought.

BERDOE, EDWARD. *The Browning Cyclopedia*. London and New
York: The Macmillan Co., 1886. Characters, titles, place names
and so on, in strict alphabetical order.

DEVANE, W. C. *A Browning Handbook*. New York: F. S. Crofts, 1935.
Enlarged second edition, New York: Appleton-Century Crofts,
1955. For long the standard handbook, and still a useful one.

CROWELL, NORTON B. *A Browning Guide*. Albuquerque: University
of New Mexico Press, 1972. The latest of the recent handbooks.

2. *Biography and Criticism*

NETTLESHIP, J. T. *Essays on Robert Browning's Poetry*. London:
Macmillan and Co., 1868. First book devoted to Browning; much
augmented in subsequent editions.

FOTHERINGHAM, J. *Studies in the Poetry of Robert Browning*. London: Kegan, Paul, and Trench, 1887. Oriented to philosophy
and religion.

GOSSE, EDMUND. *Robert Browning: Personalia*. London: Fisher,
Unwin, 1890. Reverent personal memories.

SHARPE, WILLIAM. *The Life of Robert Browning*. London: Walter
Scott, 1890. Earliest regular biography, still of interest for its
freshly constructed evaluations.

ORR, ALEXANDRA. *The Life and Letters of Robert Browning*. London: Bell and Sons, 1891. Intelligent, resourceful book more
or less authorized by the poet himself.

CHESTERTON, G. K. *Robert Browning*. New York and London: The
Macmillan Co., 1903. Didactic but intelligent critical study.

DOWDEN, EDWARD. *The Life of Robert Browning*. London: J. M.
Dent, 1904. Some interesting materials based on personal experience.

GRIFFIN, W. HALL, and H. C. MINCHIN. *The Life of Robert
Browning*. New York: The Macmillan Co., 1910. Third edition,
enlarged, 1938. Full-scale standard biography.

COOK, A. K. *A Commentary upon Browning's The Ring and the Book*.
London: Oxford University Press, 1930. Line by line commentary.

DeVane, W. C. *Browning's Parleyings: the Autobiography of a Mind.* New Haven: Yale University Press, 1927. Elucidates not only *Parleyings* but much of his other opinionative verse.

Woolf, Virginia. *Flush: A Biography.* New York: Harcourt Brace and Co., 1933. The Brownings as keyed to Elizabeth's dog Flush.

Raymond, W. O. *The Infinite Moment, and other Essays on Robert Browning.* Toronto: University of Toronto Press, 1950. Best essay explicates *Fifine at the Fair.*

Winwar, Frances. *The Immortal Lovers: Elizabeth Barrett and Robert Browning.* London: Hamish Hamilton, 1950. Exemplary item in the massive popular literature about the Brownings' courtship and marriage.

Miller, Betty. *Robert Browning: A Portrait.* New York: Scribner and Sons, 1952. Psychoanalytically oriented; eminently readable and well informed.

King, Roma A. *The Bow and the Lyre: the Art of Robert Browning.* Ann Arbor: University of Michigan Press, 1957. Good analysis of Browning's theories of poetry and esthetics.

Langbaum, Robert. *The Poetry of Experience: The Dramatic Monologue in Modern Literary Tradition.* New York: Random House, 1957. On the genre and Browning's use of it.

Honan, Park. *Browning's Characters: a Study in Technique.* New Haven: Yale University Press, 1961. Systematization of Browning's character-building processes.

Knickerbocker, K. L. and Boyd Litzinger, eds. *The Browning Critics.* Lexington: University of Kentucky Press, 1964. A collection of significant essays appearing over the years.

Litzinger, Boyd. *Time's Revenges: Browning's Reputation as a Thinker.* Knoxville: University of Tennessee Press, 1964. Fine background study.

Whitla, William. *The Central Truth: The Incarnation in Browning's Poetry.* Toronto: University of Toronto Press, 1964. Actually helps explain the shifts of Browning's total religious outlook.

Drew, Philip, ed. *Robert Browning: a Collection of Essays.* London: Methuen and Co., 1966. Overlaps the collection by Knickerbocker and Litzinger, above.

Ward, Maisie. *Robert Browning and his World.* New York: Holt, Rinehart and Winston, 1967, 1969. Two volumes, the first (covering 1812–1861) subtitled *The Private Face;* the second (covering 1861–1889) subtitled *Two Robert Brownings.* Attractive big-book biography, willfully constructed and charmingly personal in its approach.

Altick, R. D., and J. F. Loucks II. *Browning's Roman Murder Story.* Chicago: University of Chicago Press, 1968. Ten presiding aspects of *The Ring and the Book.*

BURROWS, LEONARD. *Browning the Poet: An Introductory Study.* Nedlands, Western Australia: University of Western Australia Press, 1969. Avoiding generalizations, discusses thirty selected poems in depth.

HAIR, D. S. *Browning's Experiments with Genre.* Toronto: University of Toronto Press, 1972. Very informative on Browning's technical applications of theory and idea, and on his techniques generally.

Index